CHURCH FOR T

CHURCH FOR THE CITY

•

Edited by
ERIC BLAKEBROUGH

DARTON·LONGMAN+TODD

First published in 1995 by
Darton, Longman and Todd Ltd
1 Spencer Court
140–142 Wandsworth High Street
London SW18 4JJ

This collection © 1995 Eric Blakebrough

ISBN 0–232–52086–0

A catalogue record for this book is available
from the British Library

Acknowledgements
Biblical quotations in Chapter 7 are taken from the Jerusalem Bible,
published and copyright 1966, 1967 and 1968 by Darton,
Longman and Todd Ltd and Doubleday & Co. Inc.

Phototypeset in 11/13pt Raleigh by Intype, London
Printed and bound in Great Britain by
Redwood Books, Trowbridge, Wiltshire

TO MY GRANDCHILDREN,
CAMILLE, LUKE AND ELEN

CONTENTS

•

Notes on Contributors	ix
Preface	xi

Part I: ASSESSING THE SITUATION

1. OVERVIEW OF LONDON
   Ian Hargreaves — 3

2. CHURCH MINISTRY IN LONDON
   Richard Chartres — 25

3. LONDON'S UNWANTED CITIZENS
   Eric Blakebrough — 48

4. LONDON'S RACIAL CRISIS
   Kenneth Leech — 57

Part II: ADDRESSING THE SITUATION

5. RESPONDING TO DRUG USERS
   Adele Blakebrough — 75

6. HELPING THE HOMELESS
   Sister Bridie Dowd — 91

7. CARING FOR PEOPLE WITH AIDS
   Helen Taylor-Thompson — 102

8. ACTION EVANGELISM
   Steve Chalke and Nick Page 110

9. COMMUNITY REGENERATION
   Andrew Mawson 122

10. ON NOT LEAVING IT ALL TO
    THE GOVERNMENT
    Eric Blakebrough 150

NOTES ON CONTRIBUTORS

•

ADELE BLAKEBROUGH was ordained in 1984 and is presently minister of the John Bunyan Baptist Church, Kingston-upon-Thames, and Director of the Kaleidoscope Project.

ERIC BLAKEBROUGH MBE is Pastor Emeritus of the John Bunyan Baptist Church, Kingston-upon-Thames. With his wife Mary, he founded the Kaleidoscope Project in 1968. He is author of *Permission to Be* (DLT) and also contributed to the Lent course *Meeting God Today* (DLT).

THE REVD. STEVE CHALKE is a presenter with GMTV, Director of the Oasis Trust and a minister of two Baptist churches in inner South London.

THE RT. REVD. RICHARD CHARTRES is the Anglican Bishop of Stepney. Previously he was vicar of St Stephen's, Rochester Row, Westminster, and Gresham Professor of Divinity.

SISTER BRIDIE DOWD, Daughter of Charity of St Vincent de Paul, is Director of Passage Day Centre and Night Shelter.

Sister Bridie is a qualified social worker and lives above the Centre in Westminster where she works.

Ian Hargreaves is editor of *The Independent*. Previously he was deputy editor of *The Financial Times* and Director of News and Current Affairs of the BBC. He lives in Bermondsey.

Kenneth Leech is an Anglican priest and author of many highly acclaimed books. He was formerly Race Relations Field Officer for the Anglican Board for Social Responsibility. He is currently M.B. Reckitt Urban Fellow at St Botolph's Church in the East End of London.

Andrew Mawson is minister of the Bromley by Bow URC Church. He is Chief Executive of the Bromley by Bow Centre which caters for a wide variety of community activities and is about to develop a three-acre park and integrated primary care facility. He is a Graduate of Common Purpose.

Nick Page is Director of Media at the Oasis Trust. He is the author of several books, including *Six Days*, a novel, and *George Herbert – A Portrait*.

Helen Taylor-Thompson MBE was Chairman of the Board of Governors of the Mildmay Hospital from 1985 until March 1994. She is now President and is very much involved in international efforts to care for people with AIDS.

PREFACE

•

Church leaders in London decided to make the feast of Pentecost, Saturday and Sunday, 3rd and 4th June 1995, an ecumenical celebration of the life of London. A Great Banquet on Saturday in the Banqueting House in Whitehall will bring together people from all walks of life and from different cultures and religious backgrounds. In Jesus' parable of the Great Banquet (Luke 14) the invitation to the banquet was extended to the poor and aliens in the alleys of the town and the hedgerows of the country. In enacting this parable it is hoped that we may discover again the role of the Church in relationship to local communities. A Service of Worship in Westminster Cathedral will bring together in one place Christians from the different church traditions seeking a greater sense of unity and purpose through the inspiration of the Holy Spirit. In connection with these celebrations, I was commissioned to produce this book with a view to deepening the thinking of the churches as they seek to understand the mission of the Church in London today. Although the situation being described is London in 1995, this book has relevance to Christians in urban situations everywhere as we try to fulfil God's purposes for us in the final years of this twentieth century.

A comprehensive study of our capital city would require a work of great length. I decided that what was needed for present purposes was an outline of the main features of the life of London with an assessment of some of the most pressing needs. The first chapter, by a journalist – Ian Hargreaves, Editor of *The Independent* – provides an overview of London. Mr Hargreaves emphasises the success of London as a world-class city. He outlines the discussion about how London should be governed and makes proposals for revitalising the political life of the capital. He is critical of some of the political thinking of the Church as exemplified in *Faith in the City*, but advocates an expanding role for churches in meeting the needs of local communities.

The Right Reverend Richard Chartres, Bishop of Stepney, responding to the chapter by Ian Hargreaves, acknowledges that church leaders do not always understand the complexity of economic and political issues. There is need for an informed person to keep up with social policy and prepare reports for church leaders. A review is needed of the working of the Church with the aim of fostering a better relationship between churches and local authorities, strengthening ecumenical co-operation and developing a London-wide strategy, with perhaps the appointment of a Metropolitan Bishop. Richard Chartres believes that the Christian task in London is to renew the local eucharistic communities which already exist. Christian conversion should involve the passage from a consumer-style Christianity to a sense of Christian citizenship in which every one of the faithful understands what God is calling them to be and to do.

The issues raised in the first two chapters are of more than academic interest. It is essential that in a democracy citizens are involved in the decision-making process. Londoners do not feel involved at present. It is not sufficient simply to hold general and municipal elections from time to time, to engage in occasional forms of consultation, to appoint representatives to various governing bodies: new and more dynamic forms of participation must be found, giving people more autonomy in developing their local communities.

Preface

It must not be thought that political renewal alone is the key to a better future for London. The moral and spiritual malaise calls for action. The churches cannot promote moral and spiritual well-being by telling people what to do and what not to do. Moral development takes place when people experience a benevolent social life. Unless people feel accepted, affirmed, cared for and loved, they will not develop the trust and respect which are the basis of morality. The gospel assures the believer of their acceptance by God through the life, death and resurrection of Jesus Christ, but this faith needs to find practical expression beyond the fellowship of believers. It must be the mission of the Church not only to invite individuals into the life of faith, but also to find ways of demonstrating this gospel in community projects of various kinds.

The Reverend Kenneth Leech, an Anglican priest and well-known author, works at St Botolph's Church in the East End of London. This is one of the most depressed and deprived parts of Britain where there is the largest Bangladeshi community in the world outside Bangladesh itself. There are serious problems of racism. Black and white youth in all British cities feel the impact of unemployment and the attack on social provision which has been part of government policy. Kenneth Leech is one of the best-informed people to comment on this situation and his chapter makes an important contribution.

Most people in London are unaware of the growing poverty of some sections of the population. Unemployment, homelessness, low pay, single parenthood, alcoholism and drug addiction are some of the serious social problems. But these problems are made worse by marginalising the victims of these conditions. There is need of a more positive response to those affected, from churches in particular. My own chapter is based largely on my experience of working with drug addicts in Kingston-upon-Thames over a period of twenty-five years.

The second part of the book points to ways of addressing

some of the problems of London which are within the competence of local churches. This section consists of descriptions of various church initiatives written by people working in these projects, representing their viewpoints and experience. These chapters are given as examples of church-based community work which might excite the imagination of church people as they plan to engage more effectively with their local communities.

The Reverend Adele Blakebrough tells the story of the Kaleidoscope Project in Kingston-upon-Thames which is an initiative of the John Bunyan Baptist Church. In 1967, the church discovered that its situation near to the railway station and a cluster of public houses was the centre of the drug scene in this part of London. In response to this the church began operating a club which was open all night on Fridays and catered for the late-night crowd in the town. From this beginning, Kaleidoscope has developed an integrated social-care facility and an easily accessible medical treatment programme for people addicted to drugs.

Mrs Helen Taylor-Thompson describes how a Christian community struggled to overthrow the decision of a district health authority to close the Mildmay Mission Hospital. In 1988, Mildmay opened the first AIDS hospice in Europe and its work in this field has continued to grow. In a sense Mildmay has risen like a phoenix from the ashes.

Long before Westminster Cathedral was built, the Daughters of Charity of St Vincent de Paul began work with the poor in the Westminster area. In 1980, the Sisters converted a passage in their basement into a centre for homeless people. The Passage Day Centre for Homeless People caters for 300 homeless people every day. The Director, Sister Bridie Dowd, describes the work of the centre.

The Reverend Steve Chalke is a Baptist minister who is clear about his calling as an evangelist. He is equally clear that evangelism is as much to do with actions as with words, and as much to do with social action as with church growth. Steve Chalke founded Oasis to facilitate this kind of evangelistic ministry, recruiting and training thousands of young Christians for this work. Oasis is London-based and is directed mainly at inner-city situations in England and abroad.

When the Reverend Andrew Mawson became minister of the Bromley by Bow United Reformed Church it was home to a small congregation located in one of the most deprived areas in East London. The members created from the old buildings a centre which is now a hive of activity, employing forty staff and providing a wide range of resources which include a nursery, a café and facilities to enable local people to work alongside professional artists in painting, carving, stained glass and woodwork. There are plans to develop a three-acre park and build a health centre.

There is unanimity among the contributors that non-statutory organisations, particularly churches, must fulfil a greater role in meeting many of the needs of local communities. It is now widely recognised that central government and local authorities are responsible for a framework of provisions to meet the basic needs of the whole population, but it has been found that statutory bodies are not generally the best providers of services since they are often bureaucratic, expensive, insensitive and limited by government guidelines. Non-governmental organisations have unpaid management committees, are not burdened with top-heavy administration and are small enough to be innovative and responsive to their client groups.

It has never been morally acceptable to delegate one's responsibility to the State, and the tendency to leave everything to the Government has diminished the sense of community. In situations of war, or industrial dispute, a sense of community often comes to the fore when State provision is unavailable and neighbours again begin to care for one another. Churches often facilitate such caring among members of the congregation but do not always engage sufficiently with the wider community. Cut-backs in many local services call for a much greater involvement by churches in community work. The mismatch between statutory and voluntary bodies often inhibits the expansion of the non-statutory sector which is urgently required. There is also need for a more entrepreneurial style of church ministry. These practical matters are briefly considered in the final chapter of the book.

My personal thanks as editor go to the contributors who have allowed me to pressurise them into meeting the deadline for publication, and to Darton, Longman and Todd, my publishers, who have brought my task to completion.

ERIC BLAKEBROUGH
August 1994

Part I

•

ASSESSING THE SITUATION

Chapter One

OVERVIEW OF LONDON*

●

IAN HARGREAVES

Over London, the air is thick with talk of crisis. Sir Richard Rogers, Britain's most famous architect, speaks of a London throttled by traffic, blighted by decay, robbed of vitality by lifeless commercial ghettoes. 'London,' he says, 'is simply failing to keep up with its continental counterparts.' Another group of venerable London citizens, led by Professor Sir Ralph Dahrendorf, once head of the London School of Economics and a leading European social democratic thinker, has produced a freelance blueprint for London's future, arguing that 'time is running out. London – its condition and development – is simply drifting.' Even the Confederation of British Industry felt moved in 1993 to summon the first of a series of annual conferences to address London's problems. The CBI's Director General, Howard Davies, pondered aloud whether Professor Dahrendorf was nearer the mark than Michael Heseltine, the President of the Board of Trade, who had counter-attacked against Dahrendorf with the comment that the only problem unique to the capital 'is a dire pessimism that is woefully out of place.' Mr Davies, however, had no hesitation in choosing sides. Sadly the facts seem to favour the Dahrendorf analysis, he said.

It is not difficult to support the crisis thesis with numbers, or to add to it the voice of London's poor and marginalised,

* © Ian Hargreaves 1995

who throughout history have jostled for a living alongside some of the most affluent neighbourhoods on the planet. Opinion surveys have suggested that as many as half of all Londoners would leave the city, given the opportunity, and the 1991 census confirmed that the population of greater London has continued its remorseless postwar slide, from 8.6 million in 1939 to 7 million in 1981 and 6.7 million in 1991.

Other indicators are no more cheering. The level of reported crime has increased more or less continuously in recent years. Standard mortality rates for avoidable deaths are 17 per cent higher in London than the average for the UK as a whole. Homelessness has doubled inside a decade. The Government's controversial plans to close London teaching hospitals are justified in large measure by the need to transfer resources to London's badly housed and inadequately funded general practitioner system.

Greater London's male unemployment rate, again taking 1991 census data, has been running seriously in advance of the national level (11.3 per cent) at 13.8 per cent. In inner London, the figure, admittedly at the trough of recession, was almost 19 per cent and London's poorest borough, Hackney, registered a figure of over 26. Yet next door to Hackney, in the City of London, the census day male unemployment figure was just 7 per cent and less than 15 miles away, on the south-western edge of greater London, prosperous Kingston and Richmond showed male unemployment rates of 7.5 per cent. In Hackney, on census day, no fewer than 37 per cent of economically active 16–19 year olds were without work; this age group, denied welfare benefits as well as jobs, makes up a significant proportion of the population of London's cardboard cities. The causes of London's large pockets of high unemployment are as complex as their potential solutions, but some economists feel that the almost complete disappearance of the capital's manufacturing base – only one in ten Londoners are now employed in manufacturing – has created an imbalance in the city's economy which is particularly problematic for low-skilled men.

Many other details can be added to this picture of a highly stressed, divided society. London has a fifth of Britain's ethnic minority community; 23 per cent of the population of Tower Hamlets, another chronically poor east London borough, is Bangladeshi. The national average for single parent families as a proportion of all households is put in the census at 4.18 per cent. In greater London, the figure is 5.34 per cent; in Richmond 2.9 per cent, in Hackney 9.2 per cent. Official recognition of inner London's problems has come with the successful application to the European Union in 1993 for regional aid grants to six London boroughs: Hackney, Haringey, Newham, Tower Hamlets, Enfield and Waltham Forest. Such payments have in the past been mainly associated with the derelict industrial landscapes of the north or the unique problems of Ulster.

Education is another serious concern, as the better off opt out of the state secondary education system. Inadequate public transport is a matter of concern to all social groups. Surveys in the international banking industry cite poor public transport as an aspect of London which falls far behind competitor cities on the continent. Chronic under-investment, coupled with periods of inadequate management, has made many parts of London's rail network unreliable. As a result, traffic congestion has slowed down road traffic movements; the average speed on London's roads fell from 32 kilometres per hour in the mid 1970s to 28 km/hr in the late 1980s. Meanwhile residents of inner London, only half of whom have access to a car, are the main sufferers of the related air pollution, which is manifesting itself in rising incidence of asthma. In the summer of 1994, the capital was subject to repeated smog alerts of the kind Londoners used to think reserved for cities like Los Angeles.

So far, the political response to these problems has lacked both vision and efficacy, with politicians from both major parties more concerned to fight yesterday's battles than to conceive of policy approaches relevant to present conditions.

The earthquake which apparently transformed the political landscape of London was Margaret Thatcher's decision in 1986 to abolish the Greater London Council, on the grounds that it was wasteful, superfluous and politically irresponsible. This is the schism around which party politics in the capital has since organised itself. Labour still officially favours recreating a London-wide political authority, along the lines of the GLC. At the 1992 general election, it was also Labour Party policy to abolish the Corporation of London, the ancient and exceedingly wealthy 'local authority' for London's financial district, the City. The Conservatives, meanwhile, vow that the GLC is gone for ever and that services are best delivered by a combination of London's thirty-two boroughs, the City Corporation and direct action from Whitehall.

But the reality behind this pro- and anti-GLC battle is becoming ever more complex. From the Government's side, there has been a series of policy moves designed to appease critics who accuse ministers of creating a strategic vacuum in the capital. These began with the creation in 1992 of a Cabinet-level sub-committee to oversee London affairs, which conducted its business in secret and perhaps as a result made no discernible impact on the capital's life. A more visible move was the appointment of a Minister for London Transport, although this too has been judged by some to be more shadow than substance, given the unsatisfactory dithering over major London public transport initiatives such as the channel rail link, the cross-London rail project Crossrail and the modernisation of important sections of the underground. The go-ahead for the Jubilee Line extension was a rare success.

Another initiative was the establishment in 1993 of a private-sector-led body to lobby for London's interests. London Forum has since in effect merged with London First, a similar private-sector initiative unprompted by

Government, but later charged with drafting an ambitious 'prospectus' for the capital. London First's focus in its first year was mainly upon lobbying for better transport infrastructure, although its key target, to secure political support for Crossrail fell foul of the arcane procedures of the House of Commons. More recently, London First's agenda has broadened to include inward investment, training and education and the complex array of issues which surrounds London's most marginalised citizens. The organisation's essential *modus operandi* is to proclaim and mobilise partnerships between business, local authorities and other key actors in the London scene, such as the police, trade unions and the media.

The government, however, has given the impression of running to keep up with its critics. Howard Davies, Director General of the CBI, has dismissed the Cabinet sub-committee for London as a 'non-event', and there are many in the business community who share the Dahrendorf view that a city as large and important as London cannot possibly develop dynamically and constructively without some kind of strategic, pan-London agency, and preferably one with the legitimacy which flows from direct accountability to the public. At present, for example, the only strategic body for London land-use and planning issues is the London Planning Advisory Council, a modestly funded body based in the fringe of east London at Romford and one whose recommendations the Government is free to ignore, which is precisely what it has done on a number of occasions. As a result, when LPAC, whose members include cross-party representatives from their London boroughs, declared itself, in its 1994 advice on strategic planning guidance for London, 'against almost all new road-building in the capital' and opposed the widening of the M25 and the construction of a fifth terminal at Heathrow Airport, there was no way of knowing whether this advice would have any impact at all. The likelihood was that it would not.

Labour, meanwhile, has adopted a more cautious tone

about its ideas for London. Although flushed with success at the May 1994 local elections, Labour has cooled its rhetoric about the virtues of the GLC. It remains to be seen how Labour frames its position ahead of the next general election, but the party's senior politicians are increasingly aware that at the local level, their own councillors and supporters, not to mention professional borough council officials, are increasingly responsive to ideas of partnership with the private sector. In some measure, this has been a matter of necessity, as central government has made its allocation of funds to the inner cities through a successful programme like City Challenge contingent upon the emergence of visible coalitions of interest at the local level. But it may well also represent a weakening of traditional political and institutional loyalties and a recognition that the traditional pattern of the local authority both funding and providing local services can no longer be defended as a matter of general principle. Thus, for all their failings in policy towards London, the governments of Margaret Thatcher and John Major have backed one big idea with which the tide is running: the separation of purchaser and provider roles in the public service. Although Labour has resisted this process as part of its attempt to stem the tide of privatisation, the party has in practice been forced to concede more ground, recognising that it will wish only to a limited extent to reverse this rearrangement of the boundaries between the public and the private sector.

At its broadest, the process of political change in London thus reflects forces which are reshaping political landscapes across the world, where old polarities of left and right have been rendered hazy by the ending of the cold war. These are the pressures which have produced in Italy a government led by a businessman with no political past, at the head of the party which did not exist six months before the country's general election. The same tensions have put ex-communists in power in Hungary and Poland, pledged to maintaining the momentum of a market economy. In

France, a privatising Conservative prime minister cohabits with a socialist President. In Germany, alliances have long shifted across party lines. In the United States, a new Democrat, Bill Clinton, achieves passage of key measures through Congress with tactical alliances between members of his own party and the Republicans. No longer are central political judgements determined mostly by old party lines. At the same time the established British political parties show serious signs of fatigue – Labour in the 1980s, the Conservatives in the 1990s – as the alliances of interest which formed them come under the strain of new circumstances, such as the emerging European Union, the loss of British influence overseas and the country's economic situation.

So it will increasingly prove in London. Although a Labour government may well create a lighter, leaner pan-London elected authority, it can no longer be assumed that this will resemble the GLC. Both major parties have learned much about effective local government from the Liberal Democrats, who have developed a version of community politics in London, which has involved a radical dispersal of administrative authority to local neighbourhoods. Equally, once militant left-wing councils, such as Lambeth, have moderated their stance, partly induced by the need to qualify for government programmes, but also from a widespread sense that the day of this type of politics has gone. At the same time, the most militantly Thatcherite of the Conservative boroughs, Westminster, has been chastened by a series of devastating reports from the district auditor, upholding longstanding allegations about gerrymandering and other illicit practices.

There is every indication that this less polarised political world is welcomed by the public. But it does not tell us what citizens want in any detail, or how they will establish priorities among their desires, which is the stuff of politics. In one sense, the wish-list is very clear: citizens at the local level, as at the national, want public services that work well, which are fairly distributed and which are efficient. They also want jobs, a stable or improving standard of living, freedom from the fear of crime, comfortable housing and the confidence that the education system is equipping their children to compete and be fulfilled in a rapidly changing world. They want an environment which is healthy and pleasant. In a great city like London, they also want expressions of that greatness – a tangible sense that the metropolis itself has the confidence to take on the future.

If this list sounds obvious, it also sounds a touch utopian. Cities have always accommodated extremes; it is of their nature that their very wealth will also attract the rootless, the itinerant and the mendicant. In one sense, cities must worry when they no longer possess the allure to attract society's most unfortunate. Yet it will not do to meet this agenda with a cry of 'laissez faire'. There is a public appetite for a mode of political discourse fitting to the issues at hand; there is a need for credible mechanisms of democratic accountability in the allocation of effort and resources and there is a need to shape institutions which are capable of effective responses to social and economic need.

The Church has grappled with many of these issues, most monumentally in recent years in *Faith in the City*, a report published in 1985, a year before the abolition of the GLC, and when concern about policy towards urban areas was still simmering after the inner city riots of the early 1980s. This ambitious report said much that was pertinent and proposed a trenchant and radical reordering of the Church's own priorities in urban areas. Politically, however, the report was largely a failure, in that its arguments were easily dismissed by the Thatcher government as, in effect, inadequately rigorous soft-left, soft-hearted wishfulness. Certainly, re-examining today the report's recommendations 'to government and nation', it is apparent that its authors had regurgitated without digestion a set of partisan political positions. Of the twenty-three secular recommendations, at least a dozen call for additional spending, without any attempt to gauge costs or set priorities or any indication how additional resources might appropriately be raised. If church leaders enter the domain of the political, as they should, their analysis and their proposals must withstand examination as critical as that faced by the politicians. This report in effect fell into the same trap which has bedevilled Labour's efforts to re-establish itself as a credible party of government.

At the same time, many of the report's prescriptions, although well meaning to the last comma, are shot through with an economic logic which is at best partial and at worst muddled. In questioning whether, at a time when our economy is in transition to an uncertain future, a dogmatic and inflexible macro-economic stance is appropriate, the authors certainly echoed the headline message of the opposition's political and economic stance of the day, but there was no evidence that the matter had been thought through. Likewise in its comments on the labour market and social security, the report failed to recognise any trade-off between levels of pay and benefit on the one hand and employment on the other, preferring a then fashionable aspiration towards a continental model, without again pausing to debate the possible employment effects of highly regulated labour markets elsewhere in Europe. Although the report placed a valid emphasis upon community values, warning against the Thatcherite *zeitgeist* of militant individualism, it failed to recognise sufficiently that this very individualism is in large measure a natural and irrepressible phenomenon of generally greater affluence, better education and sense of self-esteem.

These are the same forces which have led to diminished respect between the led and the leaders, but they are social forces which successful politicians and effective church leaders have to harness rather than to deny. These analytical shortcomings meant that *Faith in the City*'s concrete and valuable ideas, about the emergence of new models of partnership in the inner city, and the role available to the churches through wise use of buildings, staff and other resources, received insufficient attention.

So where do we go from here in the search for an appropriate set of policy responses towards the development of London? The first step is to establish a realistic assessment of the scale and nature of the problems, which means neither overstating nor understating them. Upon that basis, a vision can be constructed and appropriate policies conceived.

Many writers and analysts have sought to convey their sense of what makes London such a remarkable city. Spread across the Thames Valley, London has never sought to be Europe's grandest or most egotistical capital, although it was for a period the continent's most populous city; London has no equivalent of the Champs-Elysées or St Mark's Square. And yet many have found, as the American writer Henry James put it, that London offers 'on the whole the most possible form of life'. It has become a cliché that London is, in the words of A. N. Wilson, introducing a recent compendium of writing about London, 'a collection of villages slung chaotically together', although Wilson adds that paradoxically London has also been for hundreds of writers, and no doubt other citizens too, 'almost a metaphysical entity in the minds of those who contemplate it'. Wordsworth's spirit soared on Westminster Bridge; for T. S. Eliot the commuters flowing over London bridge were Dante's damned souls. William Blake, visionary and deranged, lived a mainly impoverished and nomadic life between numerous London addresses, searching for Jerusalem and sometimes finding its golden pillars rising 'from Islington to Marybone'. But did anyone ever better capture the city's power to oppress and to degrade?

> I wander through each charter'd street,
> Near where the charted Thames doth flow,
> And mark in every face I meet,
> Marks of weakness, marks of woe.

Overview of London

> In every cry of every Man,
> In every Infant's cry of fear,
> In every voice, in every ban,
> The mind-forg'd manacles I hear.

In terms of straight, descriptive insight, filtered through sympathetic eyes, it is difficult to surpass V. S. Pritchett's 1962 essay *London Perceived*. Pritchett, like so many an adopted rather than a native Londoner, rejoices in the summer view of London from Primrose Hill in north London, from which vantage point the city 'looks chiefly green . . . it is difficult anywhere to be more than 50 yards from a tree'. Indeed, a 1991 comparative study 'London: World City' found that London had more green space per square foot of office space than any of its main rivals in Europe, Asia and America, with the possible exception of Berlin. Pritchett catches with particular skill the cultural roots which are expressed in London's architecture and its way of life, its citizens' taste for privacy and their abhorrence of ostentation. He looks back to the historic conflict between mercantile London in the east (what we now think of as the City) and political and ecclesiastical London to the west (Westminster). The latter may have had its days of glory, but in Britain it has been the mercantile mind which has usually triumphed, the desire to get money, to accumulate wealth, and then as often as not to retreat to the country. 'London,' Pritchett writes, 'is before anything else the world's market.' By comparison with Paris it lacks grand architectural statements, in Pritchett's view because the mercantile mind cannot tolerate either vista or perspective. 'London,' he says, 'fails to look splendid because it is a hard place, as hard as nails.'

This may be aesthetically regrettable, but it explains a great deal about the economy not only of London, but also of Britain, dominated as that has been through most of its history by its dynamo in the south east. There is, as we well know, a flip side to this commitment to international trade and finance. Britain has never realistically entertained the option of sustained protection against imports, because to do so would have been to deny the interest of the most powerful interest groups in its own economy. That fact has in turn exposed the country's industries to very rapid adjustments to changing world conditions, which have been as painful in the short run as they may be judged inescapable in the long. These tensions are also at the root of that tense and long-running debate over the role of the city as financier of British industry. Some argue that Britain's economic focus has been too oriented towards short-term financial return, rather than the patient building of industrial structures of the kind which lie at the root of the post-war economic miracles in Germany and Japan.

Whatever view one takes about this short-term/long-term debate, it is undeniable that the financial services sector is basic to London's prosperity and quality of life. More than a fifth of Londoners are employed directly in the financial industry, which is also without question the capital's most prolific earner of foreign exchange and so the source of much of the wealth which finances the purchase of other services, which together employ a further 60 per cent of Londoners, if we take in education, health, transport, communications, distribution and leisure, including tourism. Manufacturing accounts for a mere 10 per cent of jobs and construction between 3 and 6 per cent, depending upon the stage of the economic cycle. Some efforts are under way to generate light manufacturing jobs, especially in east and north London, with the aim of redressing this anti-manufacturing bias. However, the pattern of employment growth in other post-industrial economies suggests that London will, for the imaginable future, be dependent chiefly upon services for its prosperity and its employment.

The City, however, has never had a good press; the exorbitant earnings and exclusive life-styles of its most favoured members will continue to ensure that. But Londoners should be under no illusion about this sector's importance to all of them; they should therefore have shared the City's own sense of alarm in the 1980s when it began to appear that London might be losing its competitive edge to other financial centres in Europe, much in the way that British manufacturing industry failed to hold up against foreign competition in the 1960s and 1970s. London's critics argued that the City had grown conservative, complacent and undynamic, missing opportunities to adapt to rapid changes in the global financial system, which permits investors to operate from any base around the world. London's general shabbiness and the weakness of its transport infrastructure were also compared unfavourably with the glories of Paris or the security of Frankfurt, at the heart of Europe's most powerful economy. After all, history provides examples in Venice, Genoa and Amsterdam of international financial and trading centres losing their way as rapidly and thoroughly as any manufacturing centre which loses its ability to compete on price, quality and delivery. It was for this reason that the City established in 1991 a three-year research project, designed to map London's strengths and identify threats to its position.

In reality, the City has spent a decade turbulently reforming itself. The modernisation of the stock exchange in the process known as Big Bang, the reclaiming of London's derelict docklands as a zone for offices and homes, and the internationalisation of London's leading financial firms have all gone some way to demonstrating London's will to fight back. It would be foolish to be complacent about this, not least in the light of the errors exposed along the way, from the disasters at Lloyds to the planning failures of Docklands and the stock exchange's troubled attempts to modernise its technology. But it remains true that London approaches the end of the century with its pre-eminence as a financial centre in the European time zone very much intact. This is partly a result of the City's own efforts, but also a product of London's enduring natural advantages of language, location between the American and Japanese time zones, and the fact that most foreign bankers who experience life in London's most comfortable quarters find the city calm, stimulating and civilised.

London today can still rejoice in its pre-eminence. It has over 500 foreign banks, compared with fewer than 200 in Frankfurt. The City also continues to win more than a quarter of the world's foreign exchange trading – an illustration of its ability to function as a base for UK and foreign-owned institutions. According to an interim report from the City Research Project, the only serious imaginable threat to London's future lies in the form of political risk – either some future UK government or EU action which would place London at a regulatory disadvantage compared with its international competitors. Quality of life issues will also inevitably play a part in determining the location of footloose international companies, although here for the most part London scores well against the competition. Apart from its public transport problems and the risk of further terrorist activity, London rates well against other international cities in terms of its artistic and cultural life, its ambience and the level of personal safety it still offers most of its citizens. Although scarred by recession and the related collapse in property prices in south-east England, London's economy remains a powerful engine.

It has been estimated that greater London's economy is larger than the entire economies of such EU member states as Greece, Portugal and Ireland and larger than the whole economy of oil-rich Saudi Arabia. These calculations, prepared by Douglas McWilliams for London Underground, suggest that London runs a balance of an annual trade surplus in goods and services with the UK and the rest of world of $10.6 billion (1989 data) and that Londoners and those working in London pay $8.2 billion more in taxes than is spent by central and local government in London. If nothing else, these figures indicate the importance to the entire UK of getting policy towards the capital right. They also suggest that when London Transport argues that the capital is being unjustly starved of investment capital, it has a point.

London also has many other economic strengths. It is a major tourist centre; the UK as a whole ranks fifth in the world and few itineraries exclude the capital. After a decade of transformation involving privatisation and technological advance, it is strong in telecommunications, another growing, global industry. London is also a world centre for media and advertising. Its airports are among the best and Heathrow among the very busiest in the world. It is home to the headquarters of almost half of the UK's top 500 firms, as well as being a European base for many non-European companies.

In addition, London has plenty of office space at prices which are reasonable by international standards – itself the costly result of the late 1980s boom and bust, but now an asset for the future as the economy moves into an expansionary phrase. And the capital's population is, by UK standards, well educated. Over 20 per cent of inner Londoners have a diploma, degree or higher degree, which compares with 13.4 per cent for Great Britain as a whole.

London is also a famously strong artistic and cultural base, with two of Europe's largest arts centres, two national theatre companies, five international symphony orchestras, over thirty West End theatres, two international opera houses, a world centre for art auctions and dozens of museums. *Time Out*, the listings magazine, typically lists 1500 cultural events each week. It has been estimated that 94 million attendances take place each year, in an industry which is also a significant employer (200,000 people) and source of foreign exchange earnings.

The point here is not to gloss over the realities of London's problems – the homeless, the unemployed, the marginalised, the victims of racial discrimination – but to state as firmly as possible that London has the means to address its difficulties; that it has not done so adequately is a failure of politics to harness the will of the capital's citizens to build a better city. London is not a declining city in which all must expect to share in deteriorating standards; it is a wealthy city, full of opportunity. The question is how to channel the energy and commitment of Londoners in a way that results in genuine improvement. That means facing up to difficult questions about London's politics and its institutions.

The history of governance in London is one of a troubled and never-resolved search for a balance between four sets of forces: the desire of national government in a capital which so dominates the country's life to retain control of the largest questions; the desire of Londoners for an effective and accountable pan-London body to run capital-wide services and consider major planning and strategic issues; the desire of the boroughs to retain as much local power as possible; and the desire of the City Corporation to retain its privileges and its wealth, without taking on too many additional responsibilities beyond its boundaries.

Between 1855 and 1986, when the Greater London Council was abolished, London had some form of city-wide administration, starting with a Metropolitan Board of Works aimed principally at improving the city's sewerage system. In 1889, the London County Council came into being, with powers covering sewerage, poor law, fire service, housing, transport and building control. Fifteen years later, the LCC also took control of education. Below the LCC were twenty-seven borough councils, which absorbed the responsibilities of London's parishes, which had hitherto been the smallest unit of government. As London grew and the conurbation spread well beyond the original LCC boundaries, a procession of inquiries and reforms occurred, leading eventually to the creation of the Greater London Council in 1965. The GLC was responsible for planning, main roads, refuse disposal, fire and ambulance services, traffic management and research. Education went partly to the outer London boroughs and partly to the Inner London Education Authority, and some powers, such as housing, were shared between the GLC and the boroughs. Below the GLC were thirty-two borough councils, plus the City Corporation. In 1986, the GLC was abolished, followed four years later by ILEA. Most services were transferred to the boroughs, although a rump of undistributable services were placed under the aegis of the London Residuary Body or of separate boards.

It is not surprising that London's local government arrangements were subject to constant revision. Apart from the four-way set of tensions already mentioned, London's population shifts and the impact of new transport technologies imposed a regular requirement for rethinking boundaries and the relationship between the local tax-payer base and the provision of services. The most definitive assessment of London's governance in recent years, carried out for the Joseph Rowntree Foundation in 1991, concluded that 'no system of London government has yet been capable of providing a robust and long lasting solution. It is possible that such a thing does not exist.'

Certainly the history of the last century should cause any future reformer to pause before regarding shifts in boundaries or the reallocation of responsibilities between different tiers of government as the key to improving the lives of Londoners. A weariness over such changes, many of which have been instigated by Conservative governments, is certainly now helpful to the Government in resisting calls for the re-creation of a pan-London council, although opinion polls continue to show that most Londoners still think this is necessary. But when the Government issued, in November 1993, a glossy questionnaire seeking Londoners' views on various aspects of the capital, it excluded any mention of government structure. The resulting publication was, it has to be said, anodyne and of little statistical value.

Yet the Government has not been inactive. Its establishment of a Cabinet-level committee on London has been followed not only by the promotion of London First and London Forum, but also by a move to bring together in a single London agency the main Whitehall departments whose work bears upon the city. This Office for London, headed by a civil servant, in effect brings together the former regional offices of the department of trade and industry, transport, employment and environment. It may be that this office will evolve further, becoming, in effect, a kind of department for London, dispensing London's share of the proceeds of national taxation on all matters that are above the level of the boroughs, for example subsidies to London's public transport, urban redevelopment funds, money for Training and Enterprise Councils, and so on. Even then, however, the arrangement would fall well short of any publicly identifiable body about which Londoners as a whole could express a view.

Professor Dahrendorf's idea might well point the way forward for some future government, in adding to this Office of London a directly elected executive council, responsible for public safety, transport, land use, information and promotion; 'someone who speaks with authority and responsibility on behalf of and in the interests of London's citizens and for its role as a capital city'. This body, a procurer rather than a provider of services, would have the power to raise the funds needed for its activities. The executive council would have ten or fewer members chosen by direct election and a small support staff. It would be advised on strategic and financial issues by a standing conference, consisting of London MPs, representatives from the boroughs and the City Corporation, and possibly with other co-opted members from business and voluntary organisations.

Although a number of variants on this theme can be imagined – a Mayor of London is one often-canvassed idea – the concept of a lean upper tier of London government, a purchaser not a provider and both advised and perhaps audited by a council of representatives from other democratically elected bodies, has much to recommend it. Now that the population of the UK has stabilised and that of London may well be in the process of stabilising, there may even be a chance that a new arrangement along these lines would stand the test of time, although that would depend upon the depolarisation of British politics continuing to deepen. A strengthened system of governance might also provide a forum where a renewed and practical vision of London's future could be forged.

It is certain, however, that reorganising the upper tier of London government would not be enough. If it distracted attention from more effective modes of action at the local level, it could even be damaging. Equally, there would be no point in creating a new elected London authority if it suffered alongside the rest of British local government the usurping of its powers of revenue-raising by central government. Today, after the disasters of the poll tax and as a result of further centralising impulses by the Thatcher and Major governments, only 15 per cent of money spent by local authorities is raised by them. It is hardly surprising, as a result, that the most earnest dialogue in local government is between the town hall and Whitehall, or even the town hall and Brussels, rather than between the town hall and the local electorate. One vital objective of local government, in London and beyond, is to restore financial control and a sense of responsibility to the municipality.

It is also inescapable, however, that local government, including government at borough level in London, has done much to discredit itself. The corrupt antics of recent years in Tory Westminster and Labour Lambeth are but the most extreme examples in a process which has done much to weaken public confidence and interest in London local government. At the same time, privatisation and reorganisation of essential services, such as public transport, education and the health service has created great public uncertainty over where responsibility lies for schools, family practitioner services, hospitals, buses and trains. The answer, all too often, is that responsibility lies with unelected boards, whose members are appointed from a secret list in Whitehall. Good government in London requires an opening up of this quangoised process.

There is no yearning in London for a return to centralised public hegemony over crucial services such as education or housing. There is no imaginable virtue in passing back to an Inner London Education Authority the responsibility for running hundreds of inner London schools; yet, London certainly needs the ability to plan overall levels of provision, something which can only be accomplished by some kind of pan-London body. As modern consumers, Londoners expect to be able to choose an education service which suits the circumstances of their child; they are comfortable with a mixture of public- and private-sector provision; they are happy with local school arrangements which permit serious parental involvement. A modern education system needs a uniformity of minimum standard, but a maximum of diversity of types of school. Perhaps the churches here have a growing rather than a retreating role, with the potential to reflect not sectarian and ecclesiastical divides, but the inclusion of London's diverse ethnic and religious mix. At the policy level, there is scope for placing greater power in the hands of more disadvantaged families, by basing access to school and training places on vouchers; there is much work to do in rebinding schools into their communities, making better use of expensive facilities, giving schools more freedom to set salaries, which are surely too low in the most demanding inner-city schools. A policy mix along these lines, however, cuts right across the instincts and prejudices of the major political parties; it can only be achieved if Londoners find ways of articulating their desires and the politicians respond to the freedom that is theirs in a less polarised world.

One of the first steps a reinvigorated London government should take is to devise more effective ways of consulting Londoners and letting them decide on specific issues. The citizens' initiative, the local referendum, and the expression of a range of preferences on specific issues through the ballot box (the preferendum), the use of citizens' 'juries' to examine local issues of public concern, have all been successfully deployed in other countries. London's democratic structures are, by comparison, sclerotic.

A similarly exciting and flexible approach can be imagined to any number of other agenda items in London's future. Why should there not be a referendum, for example, on whether Londoners would be prepared to levy a five-year tax on themselves and their local business in order to make a specific investment commitment, such as the modernisation or extension of part of the underground railway? Armed with such an impost, London would be able to raise the cash by borrowing in the financial markets – the type of 'municipal bond' which is an everyday event in the United States.

On housing, much has been learned from the errors of the 1960s, as well as from the mistakes that were made in the initial attempts to create free-standing Housing Action Trusts. Again, there is an evident need both to possess a strategic overview, a sense of direction, but to leave the provision of services to the neighbourhood level, giving individual tenants the maximum degree of discretion over the running of their homes and estates. Just as in education, a diversity of provision is essential, so too are imaginative financial arrangements combining the public and private sectors.

What is needed is for London to rediscover both its strategic level of government and also the parish-level locus of action, which was swept away a century ago by the modernisers of that time. What we have discovered in the last two decades is that London needs a clearer and more accountable sense of strategy than can be provided by Parliament or Whitehall, or by market forces and the London boroughs. But London also needs organisations, agencies, institutions which are close enough to the ground to understand human needs, to provide services which people want and to devise creative alternatives to the bureacratised offerings of remote public services.

In this public-private-voluntary mix of service provision,

with the public authorities concentrating largely upon the channelling of resources and the auditing of performance, the voluntary sector and the churches have a significant role to play. Two of the examples described in later chapters are well known to me – the Kaleidoscope Project in Kingston-upon-Thames and the Bromley by Bow Centre in east London. Both have done admirable work in identifying the needs of some of the most highly stressed citizens of London and developing creative responses to those needs. Their work has involved collaborating with branches of Whitehall, local government and other public agencies such as the health service. It has also involved constant battles to overcome bureaucratic rigidities and the use of charitable funding to press ahead with work that government and its agents will not recognise as valid.

This type of activity – and many other instances could be cited – offers a way for the churches to play as important a role in the reshaping of London's public services in the twenty-first century as they played in creating the services the state gradually absorbed in the nineteenth and twentieth centuries.

Chapter Two

CHURCH MINISTRY IN LONDON*

•

RICHARD CHARTRES

Cities in the Judaeo-Christian tradition are seen in an ambiguous light. The New Testament concludes with a vision of the holy city but Genesis records that the founder of the very first city was Cain. Meditations on an idealised Jerusalem – which in the past, but less so now, were frequently applied to London – alternate with eruptions from the desert margins of life as prophets enter the city like a whirlwind to purge and purify.

The Church of England has its own Rural Utopian Tendency but, as Ian Hargreaves remarks in his essay in this volume, the Church has made an important contribution to the debate about our urban future in the 1985 report, positively entitled *Faith in the City*. Whilst acknowledging the significance of the report in proposing a reordering of the Church's own priorities in urban areas, Hargreaves concludes that *Faith in the City* was a political failure built on an economic logic 'at best partial and at worst muddled'. In particular it contained numerous calls for additional spending without being precise about priorities or indicating where the necessary resources might be generated.

There is justice in these criticisms. Church leaders must be aware of the complexities involved in making choices about social provision when resources are finite and they

* © Richard Chartres 1995

must not be trapped into the dangerous luxury of simplistic calls to increase funding to defend the *status quo*.

We have to learn a new style in our approach to government and other official agencies. While it is right to seek to represent those whose access to decision makers is limited, Church leaders must speak as if they recognise that they have no monopoly on compassion and they must not fall into a mere litany of complaint. Weariness with this style within government causes many letters from Christian leaders to be marked T.O., 'treat officially', which being interpreted means 'do not take seriously'. This may explain why in recent government publications about the future of London, there is only muted appreciation of the great potential of the churches and faith communities as contributors to constructive social developments.

Often the problem is that those who have the opportunity to speak lack the leisure to master much more than the grammar of the subject. The resulting analyses and proposals are frequently not proof against the 'examination as critical as that faced by the politicians' which Hargreaves rightly urges should be expected by church leaders who enter the political domain. At a national level an attempt is made to generate adequate reflection and briefing by bodies like the Synod's Board for Social Responsibility. In a place as complex as London, however, there is an obvious need to strengthen the resources locally available to Bishops and others as they seek to discharge their responsibility to amplify the voice of those who find it hard to get a hearing.

There are a number of bodies in the field already but the Church in London needs more assistance with thinking about the relation between Christianity and the social order. Sometimes the impression is given that thinking on this issue stopped with William Temple and that the churches have not caught up with the revolution of the 1980s which has changed the landscape of London politics. A city church could be a good base for someone charged with the responsibility to keep abreast with thought in the area of social policy and to consult with fellow Christians and other practitioners in the field. Such a person should be expected to publish and give a priority to briefing church leaders, so equipping them to contribute to the debate on the future of London.

Important though it might be to participate more effectively in reflection on the various aspects of London's crisis described in Hargreaves' essay, the most significant resource represented by the churches and the other faith communities is that they are genuinely local and are present in inner-city housing estates and leafy suburbs alike. They have a potential for both participating in the delivery of social provision for the next generation and also for counteracting any growth in the polarisation of London between the suburbs and the emergent underclass. The experience of many American cities suggests that such a polarisation could have very dangerous consequences, not least for public order.

The language of partnership is on everyone's lips. In a less polarised political world the rhetoric of local authorities like Hackney has changed. Partnership with local business interests expressed through the East London Partnership has succeeded in attracting fresh resources to the borough. The problems of housing and unemployment are mountainous but they are being tackled in a more collaborative spirit. This was illustrated by the Chief Executive's recent invitation to leaders of faith communities in the borough to explore with him how they could relate to the new culture.

The meeting was part of a renewed search for community partners which has been stimulated by Government's preference for schemes in which the local authority is a procurer rather than a provider of services and concentrates on channelling resources and auditing performance. The search for community partners, however, in some of the most needy London boroughs can be discouraging. There are impressive examples of community spirit and action in east London, the part of the inner city which I know best, but local people also perceive a decay of a real sense of community.

In some respects 'community' itself has become a myth. We talk so much about it because we are anxious about the subject. In the first place there may be a number of communities in a borough which see themselves in competition with one another for scarce resources rather than as united in a struggle to improve a common home. Also, in an area where almost everyone feels marginalised and where people get used to being pushed around by impersonal economic forces and structures, there is a profound lack of confidence. Just how disabling this can be is hard to appreciate unless you have tried to build and sustain a co-operative community enterprise in the inner city. The problem is exacerbated by the economic and social stress suffered by many families. This is very serious because families of whatever shape or size are the most fundamental schools which provide an education in how to relate together. Experience of family life makes community life possible or very difficult. At the same time there has been a weakening of those traditional institutions which used to permit inner-city Londoners to make some impact on public life, notably the unions and the mass membership Labour party. Some inner-city residents feel adrift and alienated from the symbols and structures of a London which once gave them great pride. This frustration frequently surfaces. At a recent discussion in a school on the theme 'Respecting other cultures' one pupil pertinently asked, 'Well, Bish, what's my ***** culture then?'

If confidence is lacking and people face problems like the present housing shortage which seem too big for any local solutions then one of the laws of the spiritual life comes into play: if you are dissatisfied with yourself then you tend to project that dissatisfaction, sometimes violently, on to someone else. Racial groups have been scapegoated in this way.

In these conditions faith communities can have a significance far beyond anything which a count of committed members might suggest. It is hugely significant that, in areas where the motive for assembly on a public issue is most often protest, there are regular assemblies of people meeting together to praise God, to celebrate the common life and to be of service to one another and to neighbours. There are places where these assemblies offer some of the very few opportunities for people with radically dissimilar life histories and attitudes to meet one another in circumstances where friendships can develop and mutual understanding can be deepened. One aspect of the polarisation which bedevils so many aspects of London life and politics is that some ministers and politicians concerned with the problems of the capital speak and act without much personal experience of the inner city. Without the imaginative understanding of what life is like for lone parents on crime-ridden housing estates it is easy to believe that they could improve their lot 'if they were really trying'. Churches can offer the possibility of gaining this indispensable personal experience. There is a scheme in Hackney, for example, where police cadets are welcomed for weekend visits to the homes of black church members to help give young policemen and women some possibility of seeing life from a different angle.

Communities like this exist throughout the most needy parts of London. They can often generate energy in circumstances where it is easy to be immobilised by the enormity of the problems and where the exhortations of well-meaning outsiders encounter a wall of cynicism. They can also deliver services with a sure grasp of what the local constituency wants and needs. They are well placed but often they are not well organised to make the most of their opportunities for service.

The new relationship with society has in many places made the priest an increasing anomaly as the principal agent at the interface between the Church and the wider world. Parsons are not selected for their entrepreneurial talents. Many achieve astonishing things, but it is a stroke of good fortune rather than one of the fruits of good organisation to find the opportunities coinciding with the presence of someone who knows how to make things happen. There is a need for administrators and organisers to release the potential of inner-city faith communities. Part of the new approach to government agencies should be the request, 'Help us to help you achieve common objectives in the community'.

There is another factor. In recent years the statistics produced by the Church of England's Board for Ministry have revealed a trend towards the older ordinand. People are increasingly being ordained 'mid way through this darkling wood'. They bring ripe experience to the ministry, gathered in many fields but it will not be long before the youth deficit is felt throughout the leadership of the Church. Young energetic people in leadership positions attract youth and energy. The question must be asked, what is it about the lifetime project of ordained ministry which seems unattractive to so many highly motivated and gifted young Christians? Conversation with many such people suggests that they do not see themselves called to a ministry whose principal focus seems to be the maintenance of parochial structures. They are ready to respond, however, to stipendiary service which has a more diaconal character and is focused on embodying the love of Christ in social action. It would be wise to find more ways of bringing together the youthful talent that is abundantly available in Christian London and the opportunities for service which are opening up.

Two of the most acute problems mentioned by Ian Hargreaves in his survey of the nature of the crisis in London are unemployment and the continuing shortage of adequate housing. One example of what can be achieved through churches acting together with the support of official agencies is provided by the HELP project in Hackney. Nine churches have joined forces to offer training programmes to the long-term unemployed. Based at Frampton Park Baptist Church, the courses provide a combination of practical training and confidence-building exercises. Assistance is given with job searches and participants are helped to present themselves more positively at interviews.

One of the most impressive features of HELP is the way

in which it has attracted people who might not otherwise have considered joining a training course, partly by house-to-house visiting on the local estates. The churches themselves contributed a substantial sum towards the financing of the project but the lion's share came as grants from various government agencies. In the first year of its existence HELP recruited eighty-five local people, of whom thirty-two subsequently found jobs, while others moved on to further training. All this was achieved in a borough with an official unemployment figure of 26 per cent, which is generally agreed to under-estimate the real dimensions of the problem.

Faith communities have also played a creative role in responding to housing problems as part of the Housing Association movement. Here again, being a part of the wider local community and keeping alert to local hopes and fears pays dividends. The Bethnal Green and Victoria Park Housing Association is a merger between two bodies, both of which had substantial input in the early days from inner-city clergy and parish groups.

There are obvious advantages of working with the behemoths of the Housing Association world and in particular it should be the case that such organisations are able to develop new housing more cheaply, but the ability to deliver a sensible allocations policy, accessible management and efficient maintenance when the scheme is up and running is also an important consideration especially in the long term. Tower Hamlets has its share of prize-winning estates which have turned into management or maintenance headaches.

It is not surprising therefore that, in line with the rediscovery of 'the parish level locus of action' discussed by Ian Hargreaves, there has been an increasing recognition of the advantages of small-scale, locally based housing associations, many of them with church links. It is easier for such bodies to understand the social dynamics of their own patch in a way that is difficult for those who range far and wide. Local associations also have a reputation to win or lose in a defined constituency in a way that tends to make them thoroughly accountable. The accountability of bodies which provide and manage our housing stock is rightly a theme in contemporary discussions of London-wide social policy.

Allocation of housing is also obviously a crucial factor in building or destroying community. There is the imperative to attend to the needs of homeless people. There is the need to resist overt or covert racial bias. There is also, however, the need to achieve a balanced community with different age groups, family styles and ethnic origins so that a variety of strengths is available to share. That kind of balance is difficult to strike but important, especially in new housing developments. Achieving a balance requires a strength of discernment which is not easy to extract from numbers produced from some formula. Perhaps really local housing associations with good reputations for fairness have a role to play in working such a balanced approach.

Christians and other people of faith are often well placed to play a creative part in forming and focusing partnerships with a real awareness of local aspirations; funding agencies need to know how they can help faith communities to make a positive contribution to partnership building. In this connection the formation in 1992 of the Inner Cities Religious Council is a very hopeful sign. The ICRC comes under the umbrella of the Government's Action for Cities initiative and it exists to provide both the government and the faith communities around the country with a means of working together to tackle the problems facing inner-city and deprived urban areas. Members include Christians, Hindus, Jews, Muslims and Sikhs representing those faith bodies which have a substantial presence in the inner cities. Through local conferences and its newsletter 'Faith Interaction' the Council has made a good start, not least in London, in publicising good practice and in introducing leaders of faith communities to the possibility of partnership with official agencies.

Fresh resources to help churches in particular to realise

more of their potential for action in the most needy urban areas has been generated by the Church Urban Fund. The *Faith in the City* report may have had a muted political impact but it led to a fund-raising campaign in which the Church of England exceeded its target sum of £18 million. Since its inception, the Fund has channelled well over a million pounds into the most needy London boroughs to support small-scale local projects.

In the ecclesiastical world these sound like large sums but it is worth remembering that the cost of refurbishing one central London office block to modern standards can be as much as £18 million and that the budget for one medium-sized hospital is greater than the total income available to the Diocese of London. But in other respects the material and human resources the churches can bring to the service of London are impressive. Just to consider the Church of England alone, there are over a thousand parishes covering the London boroughs and distributed between the Dioceses of London, Southwark, Chelmsford and Rochester. There is an even greater number of churches and many other buildings and numerous church schools. Thousands of paid clergy and other staff are vastly outnumbered by volunteers. More than a hundred thousand adults on church electoral rolls are in touch with many more people among that 46 per cent of the population which, according to the latest Government Survey of Social Trends, still describes itself as C of E. Add to this the large numbers of Roman Catholics, who generally in inner London greatly exceed the numbers of practising Anglicans, and the Free Churches and it is possible to glimpse the astonishing potential of the churches together for the future of London. As *Faith in the City* noted, the potential of the black-led churches in the inner city is especially great. The search for community partners in Hackney cannot ignore the sixty plus independent black churches in the borough. It is a Church of England priority in Hackney to keep in touch with the leadership of these vigorous churches in the hope of being serviceable to them as they seek to have an even greater impact on the life of the whole community.

The temptation is of course to opt out of the debate altogether, immobilised by its complexity, and retreat to the ghetto of piety. This is impossible for anyone who combines a first-hand experience of some of the trends identified in Ian Hargreaves' chapter with a lively Christian faith. In the Christian tradition, spiritual life does not consist in the cultivation by the individual of ever more exquisite interior states of being. Even less does it consist in assenting to a number of disembodied, timeless propositions of a religious character. Through baptism into the life, death and resurrection of Jesus Christ, his disciples enter into the life of persons-in-communion which Christians believe is a revelation of the life of God the Holy Trinity.

Spiritual life matures as we move beyond the satisfaction of the demands of our own physical existence to an engagement with other persons. If this engagement is to be sustainable and wholesome it has to operate in three dimensions. Life in all its fullness is given to those who are related to God beyond us, to human persons beside us and to the Spirit within us. Frustration or blockage in any one of these dimensions reverberates through the others. If we are to grow we must travel around the spiral which unites these three dimensions, sustained by the self-sacrificing love of Jesus Christ.

God is love, as St John says, and 'he that loveth not his brother whom he hath seen cannot love God whom he hath not seen'. At the same time if we do not make the inner journey towards the Holy Spirit who Jesus Christ promises 'will be in you' then we shall not be free to love. If we do not negotiate along the way of our inner journey the drives and ambitions of the false self then, as so often in the history of religion, we are prone to project our anger and ruthlessness on to a God made in our own image. Furthermore, if our relation with the unconditioned God is not real then we run the risk of oppressing other human beings with the kinds of demands and expectations that are properly directed only to God. Thus we come full circle and we are ready to put out into the deep again.

Love of neighbour involves both a determination that the story and the way of Jesus Christ should be accessible and also an active concern about the circumstances which condition our lives and make us more or less apt for the life of persons-in-communion.

These inhibiting circumstances operate not only for the poor in the inner city but – perhaps more powerfully – for those city dwellers whose wealth gives them the choice to opt for a privatised life in networks of 'people like us', with neighbours kept at bay by security cameras and only glimpsed out of car windows. Poor people are more aware of needing neighbours.

Ian Hargreaves suggests that 'effective church leaders have to harness and not deny' the new spirit of individualism which is expressed by the privatised life-styles. It is certainly true that the nature of leadership has changed. Poll findings and personal experience suggest that people are less and less likely, even in the Roman Church, to listen uncritically to the voices of authority. The task of leadership in the Church of England is now like trying to take a cat for a walk. Leaders have to be constantly engaged in building consensus, and the structures put in place relatively recently with the introduction of synodical government help to only a limited extent. Some of the liveliest lay people do not wish to serve on the many committees which make up the elaborate diocesan structures. It is harder than ever for role-based committee work either to deliver an effective expression of grass-roots sentiment or to provide an effective channel of communication, but a huge amount of time and energy is absorbed in trying to continue as if the present structure were adequate.

The Church in London faces structural problems not unlike those which afflict the capital as a whole. The Church's capacity for strategic planning and action is hobbled in Anglican terms by the lack of a single focus of leadership capable of developing an overview. The four dioceses involved in London do co-operate to some extent. In particular the relations between the Dioceses of London and Chelmsford (which embraces five east London boroughs north of the Thames) have been recently translated from personal goodwill into active and specific co-operation in the area of ministerial training, though the problem of bridging the Thames remains. The Church of England could probably serve London best by adopting a London-wide provincial structure, with the responsibility for strategic issues being entrusted to a Metropolitan Bishop of London.

The days are long past, however, when the Church of England could act by itself in the social responsibility field and hope to be taken seriously. An ecumenical approach is not merely desirable but essential when tackling issues crucial to the quality of life of all Londoners, such as health care or homelessness. But again the capacity to develop a joint approach is limited by a fragmented and badly resourced ecumenical structure for London as a whole. The Roman Catholic Church also recognises the Thames as a major barrier between the Arch-dioceses of Southwark and Westminster, and there are similar Free Church divides. London is a unique case which does not fit easily into the structures devised for the rest of the country. Ecumenical structures for north London, east London and so on risk creating the kind of energy-absorbing intermediate bodies which many churches are trying to eradicate, while failing to offer the opportunity to develop a Christian voice on London-wide issues.

The other level at which Christian leadership needs to be strengthened is that of the borough; here the role of Area and Borough Deans is bound to become more significant. Efforts also have to be made to ensure that parish boundaries are more permeable and that clergy and other leaders are encouraged to work in a more collaborative way. This has often been said, but the legal structure, of the Church of

England in particular, has always made talk of 'collaborative ministry' especially between local parishes, sound somewhat utopian.

Old hands sit tight and wait for the latest surge of episcopal energy to exhaust itself and turn to wanderlust. The cynics may be wrong this time because the well-advertised financial crisis which has afflicted the Church Commissioners will have the consequence of greatly strengthening mutual accountability within dioceses. It is not the much-reported loss of £800 million which is the problem. The Church never had the money in gold doubloons under the bed; the sum represents the book value of property assets which fell during the recession. The real problem is that the Church of England has been living beyond its means for some time and in particular the pension fund is under-capitalised. The Diocese of London, which embraces only a part of the greater London area, is in the process of looking elsewhere for the £4.5 million per annum which came in subsidy from the Church Commissioners to support active ministry in the Diocese. Most of that money will have to be raised from the faithful and there are already signs that those who are paying more of the bills are demanding a greater willingness on the part of stipendiary leaders to be mutually accountable.

Structural and financial questions do not of course lie at the heart of the Church's mission in contemporary London. Obsession with these questions can indeed spell death. Tinkering with structures and fiddling with boundaries without a clear sense of the urgency of the spiritual task is the last refuge of clapped-out ecclesiastical functionaries. Likewise fundraising without vision is a recipe for continued decline.

London is one of the most significant and needy mission fields in the world. It is a great international information exchange. This is obvious at the level of the international elite who, via their computer terminals, track the progress of the American long bond and other 'securities' through the heavens from one time zone to another. It is also true in the inner city where there is a kaleidoscopic variety of different nationalities and cultures. In his book *The World City*,[1] J. Friedmann placed London first in a hierarchy of thirty such cities around the globe, using seven criteria which included population size, presence of international institutions, headquarters of trans-national corporations, significance as a financial centre, transport node, manufacturing centre and a place exhibiting a rapid growth in the business services sector.

Away from accustomed social and cultural contexts people can be open to new influences, and at a very simple level churches in London must exert themselves to be hospitable because 'some have thereby entertained angels unawares'. There are already Anglican Chaplains to the Japanese community, to Nigerian students in London and many similar initiatives. In Tower Hamlets, for example, there is a priest who after sixteen years working in Bangladesh is a fluent Bengali speaker and spends his time building bridges to the 25 per cent of the borough's population whose origins are in Bangladesh. Other churches have their own networks but again there is a lack of a strategic and ecumenically informed overview of the many opportunities to serve the international community of London.

One very salutary aspect of the presence of so many people from countries where poverty and its associated problems are so much greater is that they can hold up a mirror to the true nature of the 'crisis' in London. One thing which seems to be obvious to many newcomers to London is that there is a crisis of hope among some of the most likeable people. Sometimes this deficit of hope takes almost comic forms. A churchwarden, surveying the evidence of a rather lacklustre parish life, was moved to say, 'You know, Bishop, I think that it is only inertia that keeps us going.' In secular and religious contexts alike it is possible to hear many versions of that hopeless prayer 'Lord let it last my

---

[1] Published in 1986.

time'. London's resources are incomparably greater than those of many countries, not to mention other cities, but still it seems often that 'the best lack all conviction, while the worst are full of a passionate intensity'.

The answer cannot be found in breezy exhortations. As some foreign evangelists are discovering, it is not sufficient just to address or call London if you really want to change London. Many sensitive people inside and outside the churches are deeply concerned and genuinely puzzled about some of the social problems which manifest themselves in London in especially intractable forms. Fear of crime, for example, and debate about punishment are pervasive.

Hope used to reside in the expectation that if only we could name the problem precisely enough, then we could devise solutions in terms of stricter prison regimes, giving more resources to the police and improving the education and counselling services at every level. These are all vital topics to consider but it is hard to find any informed person who really believes that the trend of rising crime figures can be reversed by the changes which can be made relatively quickly by amending laws and reallocating resources. It may be worth doing these things anyway but it is important to recognise that the energy needed for change and hope arises from the sphere of relationships. The increase in crime and violence, certainly compounded by the long-term structural unemployment faced by large numbers of young men in the inner city, is a symptom of a breakdown in the relational world.

For many reasons we are finding it more difficult to relate in a stable way in our most fundamental school of relating, the family. One important aspect of this is that since the dawn of history every society has had to devise ways of training fathers to make a positive contribution to the business of child rearing. There is now a generation of young boys growing up in parts of the inner city with very few wholesome and available male role models to imitate.

The cult of individualism and the impossible ideal of individual self-fulfilment has obscured the way and devalued the institutions in which we grow as persons and attain fulfilment through faithful relationships. In these circumstances more savage penal regimes for offenders, far from doing any good, might actually compound the problem. It is faithful relating which gives rise to deep hope and energy.

One young former drug addict made the point very effectively as he was reflecting on his experience of four months spent in a residential rehabilitation programme in north London. He had found the community living oppressive at first. He resented the plain speaking about his attitude problems, but then he had come to see that there were those on the staff and among the other residents who were paying serious attention to what he said and did because they really cared for him. He wondered about his capacity to resist the siren call to return to the old life when he left the project and realised that he only had a chance if he kept up his new relationships. His considered judgement was delivered with almost musical but profound simplicity, 'If you wanna stay clean, you gotta stay in touch.'

Hope is not however to be invested in some simplistic cult of community. Without faith's knowledge of Jesus Christ, hope turns into the kind of utopian daydreams which have proved empty again and again. The Christian task in London is to renew the local eucharistic communities which exist already in their thousands. Too many of them at present are aggregations of people who, in a parody of the consumerist culture around them, regard the Church as an institution which ought to cater for their religious needs and feelings. Real conversion involves the passage from a consumer-style Christianity, where most of us naturally started, to a sense of Christian citizenship in which every one of the faithful understands what God is calling them to be and do in order to build the future of Jesus Christ in London. It ought not to be possible to pray 'thy kingdom come' without appreciating the cost in terms of personal commitment.

In the renewal of local eucharistic communities, the poor,

the vulnerable and the handicapped, who are present in large numbers throughout London, have a particularly important role. This role is not as objects of charitable concern but as teachers of the need to move beyond head-to-head communication and to develop the other faculties we have for heart-to-heart communication. One of the prophets of the twentieth century is Jean Vanier, who has established an international network of Christian communities in which there is not only care for handicapped people but where there is also respect for their teaching potential. Jean Vanier speaks from his own experience when he says that 'We have developed in our Western culture a high intellectualism which tells us that knowledge comes from concepts and ideas. We are frightened of the emotional and the affective. That is killing our hearts and yet the fundamental cry of human beings is for communion with others. In our communities it is the men and women with a handicap who form community. That is the mystery: that we will be healed by the poor.' The Church in London has a great potential to develop such communities but at present it must be confessed that there is remarkably little human traffic between the needy Christians of the suburbs and the eucharistic communities of the inner city.

There will be no renewal of eucharistic communities in London without the reinvigoration of genuine Christian prayer. Prayer in which we open up to the love of God in the power of the Holy Spirit by associating ourselves with Jesus Christ in his way of living and dying is fundamental to any Christian community of faith. If the churches of London are to have a future it will be because they have prayed with loyalty to Jesus Christ, with urgency and with discipline. They will have prayed for London and not merely dwelt on their own churchy concerns. Luther's definition of sin was *'incurvatus in se'* – an individual turned in upon himself. Whole churches can become similarly introverted in a preoccupation with second-order issues like disestablishment and lay presidency. Pursuit of these issues can be a displacement activity for those who are baffled by the immensity of the spiritual and missionary task which faces Christians in a world city.

There may be lessons to be learnt from the experience of some of the communities of prayer which have been established in other European cities. A call to the desert these days might well point in the direction of common prayer in the loneliness of the urban landscape. St Anthony and St Benedict left the city to build communities in the wilderness. Today's spiritual adventurers might be called to enter the city, like the community of St Egidio, established since 1968 in Rome, whose members work among poor and immigrant groups but who also give priority to daily common prayer. The realism and the infectious joy of this prayer itself has a converting power and the community has grown rapidly. Then there is the Jerusalem Community established since 1976 in the heart of Paris at the church of St Gervais. Perhaps the city of London is also ripe for such a venture.

Renewing our eucharistic communities will need leadership of a high order and this work will probably require a sea change in our strategies of ministerial formation as well a searching review of what kind of stipendiaries the Church needs to take advantage of the many opportunities which are opening up.

Ministerial training has been dominated by a rationalistic mindset which has tended to see 'the faith' as a package of propositions which can be communicated mind to mind. Ministers therefore have been encouraged to take more time out of life in order to learn more things from books. Reflection upon the Christian experience does indeed suggest a number of propositions which it is important to express as clearly and precisely as possible. Jesus Christ, however, did not say that he had come as a teacher of religious truths, he said, 'I am the way, the truth and the life'. He did not write a book to abridge his ideas or reduce them to a system; he saw his future in a community of disciples who were to 'do this in remembrance of me'.

The Church of England dioceses in London have embarked upon two new essays in ministerial formation, one north and one south of the river. The North Thames Course, founded by a partnership involving Oak Hill College with the Dioceses of Chelmsford and London, has as part of its rationale the conviction that the future ministry of the Church in London needs to be given a theological formation which is more profoundly rooted in the life of parishes and local eucharistic communities. This could also have a vitalising effect on the parishes involved, as teachers are taught and encouraged to participate in rigorous theological reflection on the work they are doing.

In the past it has sometimes been the case that candidates recruited from the ministry in the inner city have been sent off to a training agency in a leafy cathedral city which, in order to fulfil the demands of the national church, then sends the same candidates to study the inner-city conditions in an out-station in a Midlands conurbation. Now there is a determination to mobilise more of the huge resources for ministerial formation in London itself in a strategy which recalls some of the recommendations in the *Faith in the City* report. At the same time more serious attention must be given to the development of that faculty which in the patristic period was called 'the heart'. Ministers must learn to pray 'with the mind in the heart' and develop that capacity to engage with truth embodied in a person and not just with truths presented in a package.

There will be fears, which deserve to be taken seriously, that this 'contextualised' approach is a cloak for abandoning intellectual rigour in the study of scripture and theology. It would be a tragedy if this were so since the capacity of the Church in London to contribute from its own tradition to debates about the social and economic order will depend on a new generation of more comprehensively educated theologians. The secular universities in London produce well-trained scholars in a number of sub-disciplines in theology and Christians ought not to ignore the resources still available in universities. Faculties, however, cannot limit their appointments to believers and the courses they offer have to satisfy the requirements of a rather narrow definition of academic respectability. In the battle for the heart and mind of London, the churches ought to be giving serious consideration to the establishment of a spiritual university where theologians can be formed in a community of prayer and in an ecclesial context.

One great stimulus to urgent study in London is the welcome presence of so many Christians from other cultures with a very different way of relating to the apostolic tradition, and also of representatives of all the great world religions. In future it may be seen as part of the work of Providence that so many Asian and Afro-Caribbean Christians have come to settle in London. The indigenous Church has much to learn from the commitment and spiritual wisdom of Christians from other continents. Through intermediaries like the south-London-based Simon of Cyrene Institute it should be possible to devise more occasions and opportunities where the Asian and Afro-Caribbean experience can be shared with the host Christian culture. This work has hardly begun.

Likewise there is the potential in London for the profound learning which occurs when faiths encounter one another in an atmosphere conducive to deep mutual attention. The idea that all faiths are talking about the same God and you can just pick and mix the best aspects of Islam, Buddhism and the rest is in fact a new-confected religion and a rather shallow one. Dialogue with other faith traditions on the basis of mutual respect is often a way of understanding with fresh clarity the unique quality of the revelation of God in Jesus Christ. By contrast, however, the commitment of many Muslims in the inner city to the life of prayer and their incredulity at the lukewarm way in which many Christians practise their faith is a judgement on a Laodicean Church. Islam is making English converts in London from people impressed by the strength of a faith whose five pillars of practice unite Muslims from Ilford to Isfahan. Islam could soon become a major British religion and this should not cause hysteria among Christians but it should alert them to the urgency of missionary work among the millions of nominal Christians in such a strategically significant international information exchange as London. The 1988 Lambeth Conference declared that 'the dominant model of the church within the Anglican communion is a pastoral one ... The pressing needs of today's world demand that there be a massive shift to a mission orientation throughout the communion.' This declaration is still one which London Anglicans, with one or two honourable exceptions, need to find means of translating into the way they allocate their efforts and resources.

The challenges and opportunities of London point not only to a new style of ministerial formation but above all to a more profoundly evangelised Church in which everyone is gripped by the living truth that it is by baptism that we are all commissioned as active and responsible citizens in the Church of God. Some churches have become good at inviting their neighbours to consider the claims of Christ but fewer have developed really profound programmes for incorporating growing Christians in the mystery of Easter in a way that transforms their lives and sets them free for adventurous Christian service. The Early Church had such a process before the mass conversions of the fourth and fifth centuries caused a modification of practice. The vestiges of this profound incorporation in the Paschal mystery survive in our observance of Lent. As even the memory of Christendom fades, every church will have to consider again its strategy for assisting growing Christians to become in deed and in truth 'very members incorporate in the mystical body of our Lord Jesus Christ which is the blessed company of all faithful people'.

The implicit strategy of the Church of England seems to have rested on the assumption that everyone acquired the grammar of the Christian faith at school, amplified for some by Sunday School provision. Inevitably many people move away from the Church during their teenage years but one of life's crises or climacteric events will find them returning to the church on the corner and feeling sufficiently at home there to be able to grow through the normal means of sermons and liturgical worship. The experience of nearly every minister is that, despite the best efforts of Education Secretaries, more schools have found it hard for some decades past even to impart the grammar of the Christian faith. This is in part the consequence of a worrying shortage of good Christian teachers. In these circumstances every church needs to be a catechetical environment, able at every level in collaboration with neighbours to 'equip the saints' for their work. Places like Holy Trinity, Brompton and St Helen's, Bishopsgate are showing the way, but elsewhere the work has hardly begun.

In the discussion of the concept of the city in his book *The Etymologies*, St Isidore of Seville treats the subject under the aspects of *urbs* and *civitas*. The word *civitas* draws attention to the emotions, rituals and convictions which cohere in the community of the city. *Urbs* stands for the built environment to which, thus far, I have paid little attention. *Urbs* and *civitas* clearly have a bearing on one another.

We are living in a post-Christian era, but still St Paul's is a universally recognisable symbol of London as well as of Christian faith. From Roman times the City of London has developed around significant Christian shrines. Churches which 'robe our destinies in stone' still evoke strong emotions even among non-attenders and they remain very significant in the Church's missionary effort. Dilapidated church buildings signal the decrepitude of faith with terrible eloquence. The beauties of a church by Wren or Hawksmoor signal that there are other values in the world besides those that are dominated by considerations like price per square foot. The steps and columns of St Paul's are a reminder and an invitation to participate in a public world to which every member of the community has access. By contrast, the Lloyds building presents its backside to the public world and reserves its shining face for the opulent privacy of the interior.

Not all Christian leaders, and not even all bishops, are members of the Goth and Vandal tendency who dismiss the significance of the built environment and regard churches as no more than disposable plant. In London, however, Christian leaders have to live with the reality that there are not enough resources to preserve everything. At the same time if conservation doctrine becomes so inflexible that it puts a full stop to developments in church interiors of the kind that have happened in every age before this one, then inner-city congregations are likely to abandon their building to vandals of a more contemporary kind. English Heritage has shown heartening signs of being alert to the gravity of the situation and it is obvious that a strategic plan for London needs to be prepared to bring together the interests of those whose primary focus is the architectural heritage with those whose priority must be the gospel. These interests are not mutually exclusive and the best allies of the conservationists are the communities of faithful people who over the centuries have preserved a large part of what we all value in the streetscape of London. The churches remain while so much else disappeared in the orgy of post-war redevelopment.

London has always stirred strong emotions. For some, like Shelley, 'Hell is a city much like London – a populous and smoky city'. For others faith generates hope and makes it possible to echo the words of the London seer Blake:

> And now the time returns again:
> Our souls exult, and London's towers
> Receive the Lamb of God to dwell
> In England's green and pleasant bowers.

It is a good time to be working for the future of Jesus Christ in London.

Chapter Three

LONDON'S UNWANTED CITIZENS[*]

●

ERIC BLAKEBROUGH

London can survive with high levels of poverty, homelessness, crime and racial tension. These problems are concentrated in a few districts, but not too much so; rather they are distributed throughout greater London and do not generally disfigure the life of the city.

London's East End is traditionally thought of as an area of poor housing, of high levels of crime and racial tension. But most of the pre-war slums were demolished in the London Blitz, and although some badly designed post-war estates remain, there are new estates of two- and three-storey houses which are indeed pleasant. Even in boroughs such as Tower Hamlets and Hackney where unemployment rates hover around 20 per cent, with 23 per cent of the population dependent on income support, the great majority of people are enjoying a good standard of living. Many artists choose to live in Tower Hamlets and many intellectuals choose to live in Hackney. A number of the people who work in the stock exchange live in London's East End, where people have traditionally been market orientated.

The Royal Borough of Kingston-upon-Thames is generally affluent, and although hit by the recent recession, unemployment is in single figures in terms of percentage of population. But while cars queue to get into the multi-storey car

[*] © Eric Blakebrough 1995

parks, and people throng the Bentall Centre and the John Lewis Store, there are poor people in Kingston, including a number of young unemployed people who have turned to drug misuse.

In some London boroughs, unemployment among young men exceeds 45 per cent; over a quarter of the Pakistani/Bangladeshi population in London is unemployed; in some parts of London over 60 per cent of young black people are unemployed. The majority of Londoners commuting from the suburbs into central London are unaware of the people represented by these statistics. Frankly, the well-off majority of Londoners do not need the poor minority; they do not know them, or care much about them. In this way the poor are isolated, and since they are a minority in most boroughs they have no political power.

Croydon, with a population of 350,000, is a good example of a London borough which is mainly prosperous, with a thriving shopping centre, affluent suburban communities and areas of urban decline which are hardly visible to the majority of the residents in the borough.

Public opinion is in favour of greater expenditure on services such as education and health which benefit all sections of the community, but there is noticeable hostility towards the homeless, single parents and the unemployed.

The idea that people could enjoy complete security from the cradle to the grave was never realistic. Mortality is experienced in every part of life – it is impossible to bring wholeness to every broken situation. That is the truth in the statement of Jesus: 'The poor you have always among you.' To think that the State could take over responsibility for the total welfare of every citizen is absurd. The collapse of Communism in the former United States of Soviet Russia and her East European satellite states dramatically illustrates the economic impracticability of a system intended to level out the ups and downs of individual fortunes. Christians have always sensed the idolatry which gave the State omnipotence.

The dawning of this realisation gave Thatcherism its credibility in the 1980s. However, Thatcherism went too far. When Margaret Thatcher declared that there is no such thing as society, it became clear that she was abandoning the post-war consensus that citizens should have mutual responsibility for each other. The nation had not forgotten the vow made by many at the end of the war that there should be no return to the old days when everybody was expected to fend for themselves, with sections of the population experiencing unemployment, inadequate housing, poverty in times of adversity, limited access to good medical care and low standards of education for the children of working-class parents. Suddenly, Margaret Thatcher became unpopular; so much so that even her own party turned against her. Since then the Conservative Party has vacillated between the radicals who want to press on towards individual libertarianism with only minimum standards of state provision, and others who believe that we should preserve the main elements of social provision in order to achieve a nation at ease with itself.

In the meantime, compassion is a virtue in short supply. There has been a vicious attack upon the most vulnerable members of society. The homeless are depicted, in the main, as wilfully rebellious youngsters who have run away from their parents, or who are the products of parents whose irresponsibility is the result of too much state welfare! Single mothers are stereotyped as women whose reproductive profligacy is to be blamed on the failure of the Church to preach morality. Rising levels of crime are attributed to wickedness which has grown in an age when parents have neglected their responsibilities, teachers have not insisted on proper discipline and senior churchmen have failed to condemn sin. The poor no longer exist in Britain today, it is claimed; there are only relatively poor people who should stop asking for more.

Unemployment has risen sharply in London in recent years. Over a third of manufacturing jobs lost in Britain in the decade 1980 to 1990 were in London. In recent years there has been a similar fall in the number of jobs in the construction industry.

But what is the public perception of the problem of unemployment in London? It is claimed that most of the unemployed are only short-term unemployed who will be back to work as soon as the cyclical upturn in the economy occurs. Others, it is suggested, should make a greater effort to find work. It is proposed that unskilled workers should be made to take uncongenial work, with limited state provision to supplement poverty levels of pay.

Among the more successful members of society there is a certain satisfaction with the way things are and a degree of bewilderment as to why there is not a greater 'feel good' factor apparent in the nation. The fact is, there is widespread fear of unemployment as every day more redundancies are declared; the increase in jobs is not seen to be an increase in good jobs, but an increase in part-time jobs, poorly paid jobs and insecure jobs. Enterprise needs to be encouraged and efficiency is desirable, but when the pressure is on to the point of creating great insecurity for many people, then those who are enjoying the competition ought to take notice of the pain of those who are struggling.

People created in the image of God are made to be creative. Real creativity demands great effort. For these reasons a competitive society is necessary. But the effort to be made should not be concerned solely with personal fulfilment. The Christian gospel is that God gives himself for the salvation of the world. This sense of concern for the good of others should be an essential part of human endeavour.

There are present day prophets who question the goal of all our striving. Professor Charles Handy, of the London Business School, in his recent book, *The Empty Raincoat*,[1] writes, 'It is easy to lose ourselves in efficiency, to treat that

---

[1] Hutchinson, 1994, p. 1

efficiency as an end in itself and not a means to other ends.' It is important to strive for greater efficiency if we are to meet people's needs. But in the present climate, the benefits of greater efficiency are being swallowed up by huge increases to some top executives, rewards for the exceptionally brilliant and increased profits to shareholders. There is too little reward for those achieving greater productivity at the lower levels of the work force.

There needs to be greater efficiency in public services, but the public perception is that the purpose of the drive for greater efficiency is to provide tax cuts to win elections and benefit the better off. There is little good news for the poor.

The crucial debate today needs to be about the proper balance between the operation of the market and the social needs of the population as a whole. This is not only a matter of legislation, it is also about the creation of a more socially responsible business culture. It is shabby practice to exploit high levels of unemployment by paying such low wages that the taxpayer has to make up the deficiency by income support and similar benefits. A person who works hard has a right to a living wage. 'The worker deserves his pay.' (Luke 10:7)

It is also bad practice to reduce expenditure on proper skills training, simply pay a little more to cream off the available talent and leave it to other firms, or the Government, to bear the cost of training. Furthermore, firms should allocate a realistic proportion of profits to efforts to improve the environment and to support socially valuable enterprises. Such philanthropic activities should not be features of certain well-known companies; they should be general practice. Unfortunately, such a socially responsible business culture is unlikely to grow spontaneously. It requires legislation such as that provided in the Social Chapter proposed by the European Union, to encourage these developments. The meanness which has characterised some political pronouncements recently promotes hard and narrow-minded thinking among business executives.

The continuing trend in Britain of the rich getting richer and the poor getting poorer is particularly visible in London where there are areas of luxury housing near to ghettos of poverty, and where top-class restaurants are only a short distance across Waterloo Bridge from the cement walkways where the homeless are to be found in Cardboard City. It is not the case that money spent on improving the lot of the poor is wasted. I spent over twenty-five years in London working with drug users, whom many regard as the dregs of society. My experience convinces me that decent facilities and a good environment are essential to personal development. Cut-backs in public building programmes can be detrimental to the health and wealth of communities.

Without a vision of the New Jerusalem, we will create a divided and disillusioned society. Once people are disillusioned, morality collapses and all manner of social ills break out. The experience of Russia illustrates not only the fatal flaw in State Socialism, the present breakdown in law and order shows the evil consequences of widespread disillusionment. If we are to avoid the frequent sound of police sirens in certain districts of our cities, we must divert an increasing proportion of the rewards of greater efficiency to programmes of urban renewal. We have had too many short-term, 'pump-priming' programmes; we need the kind of sustained effort that a householder needs to make to transform a building site into a home and garden. It is uplifting to see the transformation of Docklands, but it is shameful to see the neglect of many of our inner-city schools and areas of poor housing. Deregulation giving more freedom to entrepreneurs must not be allowed to lead to less equality, more misery and new areas of deprivation.

The needs of the poor are little understood by most people. Executives travel mainly through the better parts of the city by private car or taxi; they are seldom inconvenienced by beggars. Even middle- and low-income workers have only vague and ill-informed impressions of growing poverty in parts of London.

Howard Davies, Director General of the CBI, in a speech recently challenged both employers and the Government to respond to the needs of the new poor. He drew attention to the fact that over the past twenty years the total number of one-parent families in Britain has risen from just over half a million to 1.3 million in 1991. The economic fortunes of most of these households depend on the employment prospects of women. And the prospects for many of these women are bleak. If a single woman has been in work with the same employer for at least two years, when she has a baby she will receive £52.50 a week in statutory maternity pay. If unemployed, she will receive a one-off maternity payment of £100.

When the Housing Benefit rules were changed in 1988, a million people lost their right to this benefit and five million others had it cut. When a poor family defaults in paying electricity, water or gas bills, it is usual to install meters. When money is short, the family is left in the cold and dark, and may even have the water supply turned off. If they live in London, they cannot light a wood fire to cook or warm themselves. Many of those in bed and breakfast accommodation have no proper laundry facilities and may be forced to use expensive launderettes.

The National Council for One Parent Families says that financial hardship has become the overwhelming reason why women ask for their children to be adopted. Others, who cannot cope and cannot bring themselves to have their children adopted, develop a love-hate relationship with a social worker, half wanting their child taken into care and half feeling angry at seeing no other alternative. I have often observed increased use of drugs by mothers facing this cruel dilemma.

The breakdown of marriages is happening in all sections of society. It is not a phenomenon confined to the poor and reckless, although poor families are subjected to greater destructive forces. As the poor have been forced to live in certain districts, their plight has become more visible and increasingly they are being stigmatised. This has enabled the Government to cut benefits and remove priority in housing, without too much protest.

Employers can help by making more flexible arrangements for the employment of women. The business community can also help provide more child-care facilities. The Government should stop implying that most of the poor have only themselves to blame. Whatever changes may be necessary to stop people exploiting loopholes in the benefits system, it should be the priority of Government to alleviate the high levels of poverty existing in Britain today.

A symptom of the disease in our society is the continuing rise in illicit drug use. Professor W. J. Wilson, a distinguished African-American scholar, has described the collapse of social institutions under the stress of poverty in inner cities. In this context he shows how young people faced with no real prospects turn to an alternative culture of drug-trafficking and crime. My experience of working with illicit drug users in London convinces me that there is no simple analysis of the reasons why people become addicted to drugs. A lack of prospect of success in mainstream society is not the most important cause of drug dependency, but it is one of the significant factors. It is also my experience that a lack of employment opportunities and homelessness greatly exacerbate the problems of drug addiction and make rehabilitation much more problematic.

The seriousness of the drug problem in London can hardly be exaggerated. Some heroin addicts pay for their habit by means of prostitution and drug-trafficking, but the majority must find up to £80 a day from other crime to purchase a gram a day of heroin. Calculating the potential cost of £80 per person per day, and taking into account that stolen goods are unlikely to fetch more than a third of their retail value, a working party of the Greater Manchester Police concluded that each addict has a yearly 'crime potential' to steal almost £90,000 worth of property!

Drug treatment centres supplying methadone as a substitute for heroin greatly reduce this criminal activity. The use of methadone under medical supervision provides a safe dose of a pure drug. The slow-acting properties of methadone enable an addict to function without the extreme mood swings which occur with taking frequent doses of heroin. Unfortunately, many doctors who by custom think hopefully in terms of curing addiction are not enthusiastic about methadone maintenance programmes. In this respect, the Government's Advisory Council on the Misuse of Drugs has shown more realism in accepting harm reduction as a valid goal and has adopted a pragmatic approach to the problems of illicit drug use.

It is easy to denigrate the poor, the homeless, the unemployed, single mothers, drug addicts and all those who exemplify the serious social problems in our cities. The majority of voters are unconcerned. Social commentators are dismissed as wrong-headed. Politicians have other priorities. The Church has the independence and divine vocation to speak out against poverty and injustice. But it is not good enough simply to condemn, it is required of local churches that they become much more involved in relieving the suffering which exists near to their doors. In this matter, actions speak louder than words.

Chapter Four

LONDON'S RACIAL CRISIS*

•

KENNETH LEECH

PERSONAL AND POLITICAL

The word 'crisis', which I have used in the title of this chapter, suggests both threat and opportunity. The biblical word *krisis* implies, and is usually translated as, judgement. It can be a prelude to disaster; it can also be the moment of truth, of decision, of turning. It can be what in biblical terms would be called a *kairos* moment. There are two words for time in the Bible, *chronos* and *kairos*. *Chronos* (from which we get 'chronology' and 'chronological') means linear time, when one minute follows another in sequence. But *kairos* means time as a moment of decision, a crisis moment, a time of choosing. From time to time in the life of human beings and human societies, a challenge faces us which presents us with a fundamental choice between life and death, hope or futility, good or evil. I believe that our present predicament about race is such a moment. If it passes us by, the challenge to think and act in a new way could be lost. If the wrong response is made, if the warning signals are ignored, we will reap the whirlwind. At a time when in South Africa, for many years the only fully racist state in the world, a new way forward is being found,

* © Kenneth Leech 1995

London's failure to respond creatively would be terrible and tragic.

For me the slogan 'The personal is political' is central to the challenge before us. The slogan can also be reversed: 'The political is personal'. To try to understand both the importance and the dangers inherent in this slogan, either way round, is nowhere more urgent and more helpful than in the encounter with racism, that ugly word to describe an uglier and dangerous reality in the life of London and other cities.

Clearly racism must be tackled, where it manifests itself, at both the personal and the structural levels, but it is a serious error to reduce all racism to the level of personal prejudice or personal transformation. Many Christians, afraid of what they see as the contamination involved in political work, are particularly prone to the temptation to reduce all action to the personal. What is often called 'identity politics' is necessary but inadequate. The political is always personal but it cannot be reduced to the personal; the personal is always political, and the interaction between these two levels of existence must be maintained if we are to act effectively. The response of the Church to the racial crisis depends on its ability to negotiate this ambiguous area.

For me, the politics of race and racism is personal in a very specific sense. It is thirty-seven years since I first arrived in the East End of London as a student. I lived in Cable Street, scene of the famous anti-fascist battle of 1936. A reactionary Labour Party was in power in Stepney, with three Communists – Solly Kaye, Barney Borman and Max Levitas – and one Independent on the council. A small black community, strongly ghettoised, lived in the Cable Street district, known locally as 'the coloured quarter'. The political machine took no notice of them. There were no black members of the Labour Party, and it had the depressing atmosphere of a party long past its peak. As late as 1982, nineteen of the forty-three Labour Councillors had been there for twenty years or more – one of them, Joe O'Connor, since 1928! The power base of Labour had been built on the docks. But membership of the party had been declining for years, as had confidence in its ability to act for the people. So by the 1980s this multi-racial community, where one in four of the population was black, was still represented by elderly white men.

On the edge of this multi-racial community, mainly in Bethnal Green, was some residual organised fascism. The early fascist movement, led by Sir Oswald Mosley, was strong and dangerous in the 1930s, and the East End was the focal point for its campaign. The fascist presence never went away, and Mosley himself stood as parliamentary candidate for Shoreditch and Finsbury as late as 1965. The strongholds of the Mosley movement – Bethnal Green, Stepney, Limehouse and Shoreditch – remained fertile ground for the newer groups. In 1958 there was some concern that the activity of fascist groups in North Kensington might spread to the East End. Just before I arrived in east London, a local branch of the National Labour Party – which later merged with the White Defence League to form the British National Party (not the same group as today's BNP) – had been formed at the Carpenters Arms in Cheshire Street. The BNP sold its newspaper *Combat* at the corner of Cheshire Street and Kerbela Street, Bethnal Green, during the early 1960s. The BNP merged with other groups to form the National Front in 1967. The NF was active in the East End during the 1970s, reaching the peak of its activity in 1978. After the decline of the NF following the general election of 1979, when their vote collapsed virtually everywhere, there was a fragmentation and regrouping within British fascism. The NF split into various groups, one of which, led by John Tyndall, became the present BNP in 1982. Into this new group came members of earlier fascist organisations. It is the BNP which has formed the main fascist presence in the East End since then.

All this is part of my own personal history. These streets,

these struggles, have shaped my life and consciousness. I cannot be neutral about racism. It makes me very angry, very passionate, and I need – we all need – to direct that passion in the most effective ways if we are to help bring this evil to an end. But passion needs to be united with accurate knowledge and severe mental discipline. Local churches, in their encounters with structures of evil in society, must be armed with detailed information and sound analysis as well as with zeal for righteousness.

THE 'NEW MINORITIES'

We cannot understand the position of minorities in London unless we see them within the larger framework of urban developments and shifts: economic restructuring, the increasingly sharp contrasts between wealth and poverty, the spread of gentrification and 'yuppification', the increase in housing stress, homelessness, and so on. Much of the media coverage about race in the 1960s consisted of sensational articles on 'the dark million' or 'the alien invasion', while a good deal of recent treatment of racial inequality has abstracted race from issues of inequality and deprivation as a whole. Racial inequality, while it possesses concrete and specific features which cannot be reduced to other terms, can nevertheless be understood only in the context of inequality and exploitation within the mainstream social structures. Constantly, and increasingly, the problems of the ethnic minorities in London expose, and often present in magnified form, problems which are present throughout the capital.

In part this is because the black minorities are more heavily concentrated in the urban areas than is the population as a whole. They are thus simultaneously more visible and more invisible: more visible, because their presence in areas of stress helps to portray them as the unique victims, and even as the creators, of that stress; invisible, because, since half of the white population, including many of those in positions of power in the urban areas, live in districts with no black people, they can be ignored in policy decisions and national institutional strategies.

According to the most recent data, 50 million of Britain's 54 million population were born here. Ninety-four per cent are white. Black minorities comprise around 6 per cent of the population. Of these, 51 per cent are of Asian and 19 per cent of West Indian origin. Thus, in spite of the increases due to post-imperial migration and natural increase, we are referring to a very small section of the population. Their distribution broadly follows lines which were determined in the late 1950s and early 1960s. Black minorities are heavily represented in the South East and well represented in the west and east Midlands, the North West and Yorkshire, but comprise only around 3 per cent of the population in Scotland or Wales. Ninety per cent of the black population live in the big five metropolitan regions, in contrast to three-quarters of whites. Moreover black communities in London, as in every urban conurbation, are more heavily concentrated in the inner cores than is the white population. Thus 70 per cent of Asians and 81 per cent of Afro-Caribbeans live in 'inner city' districts, in contrast to only 31 per cent of whites.

In inner London, non-white people form around 25 per cent of the population. In Brent they form 45 per cent, in Newham 42 per cent, in Tower Hamlets 36 per cent, and in Hackney 34 per cent. London itself is a complex structure and it is dangerous to generalise. However, a number of aspects of the racial climate have been very noticeably important in recent years.

THE STRUGGLE FOR HOUSING

It is over thirty years since 'the Profumo affair' brought Perec Rachman into the public realm. These were the years when 'No coloureds, no Irish, no dogs' signs were seen in the windows of London boarding houses. Rachman was the main landlord for the black community in London. (The term 'Rachmanism' is now in the Oxford English Dictionary as a term for housing racketeering.) As we look back on 1963 we see that none of the issues has been adequately tackled: indeed every one has become more serious. Maldistribution of housing was a problem in 1963. The decline in cheap private rented housing has intensified. 'Gentrification' (a term coined by Ruth Glass at the end of the 1950s) has continued to squeeze out poor people from many parts of inner London. The numbers of homeless people have continued to increase. While the cruder forms of racial discrimination in housing have been removed, all recent studies have shown that discrimination and disadvantage remain deeply entrenched. The geography of racial disadvantage, a geography which was well in place by 1963 – and to which Rachman's activities contributed a good deal – remains essentially as it was in the early 1960s.

The claim made by the Milner Holland Report on London's housing (1965) that black people expose the inequities and distortions in the housing market as a whole remains true. Since then London's housing crisis has deepened, and black people share disproportionately in that crisis. Many aspects, such as the allocation of local authority housing, are well documented. Others, such as the racial dimensions of housing investment, remain fairly neglected by researchers. At present nationwide some 52 per cent of Asian and 15 per cent of Afro-Caribbean households have to share basic amenities. Residential segregation has intensified, and every Housing Act since the mid 1970s has sustained segregation and reduced the residential options for black people. Increasing numbers of black people suffer from overcrowding and homelessness. In London particularly there has been a 'racialisation' of deprivation. The Spitalfields ward of Tower Hamlets in which I work is the most overcrowded ward in the UK: it contains the largest Bangladeshi community outside Bangladesh. At the same time it needs to be recognised that housing stress among black residents is one example, a dramatic example, of the housing crisis of London as a whole.

POVERTY AND RACE

Black people are scattered throughout the class structure. Most poor people are not black, many black people are not poor, and there is a black middle class, though its size and significance are often exaggerated. The Asian community (which comprises 4 per cent of the population) provides 25 per cent of doctors, almost 10 per cent of accountants, and just under 50 per cent of retail traders. There are no close parallels in London to the vast ghettoes of American cities where poverty and colour are highly correlated. However, we have certainly seen the emergence in recent years of a community of poor black people. This group is often called 'the underclass', an imprecise term taken over from American sociology with the suggestion of long-term entrenchment and with undertones of contempt. The proportion of poor black people has increased as black communities in all inner cities have been hard hit by unemployment. Yet across the board in London, poverty, among black and white, is increasingly a phenomenon of the young and of families.

For the vast majority of the British population, most of whom reside outside inner cities, the urban poor, black and white, remain invisible. But in momentary phases they reappear. So the panic around the size of the black population was both reflected and strengthened in Margaret Thatcher's 'swamping' interview of January 1978 in which she claimed that the British culture was in danger from an alien wedge. Media coverage of the 1981 and 1985 rebellions and disturbances in many inner cities fed the ill-informed fears of white communities, linking protest with crime and disorder so that these came to be seen as the cultural characteristics of black people. There have been similar reactions prior to the Notting Hill carnivals when newspapers complained of black youth 'steaming' or 'ironing' the pockets of the hard-working white city workers in London's tubes and streets. So the growing numbers of young black poor are the vehicles of the government's crisis of social control. The discourse around 'the underclass', like that around 'the family', is part of an attempt to explain the destruction of the fabric of society. Christians, black and white, need to be very astute and very careful in how they respond to this discourse with its clear racial dimensions. The role of spiritual ally to the culture of Babylon is not one which we should accept, but to resist this seduction requires resources of spiritual perception and political commitment.

RACIAL VIOLENCE AND HARASSMENT

Racial violence has been a feature of London life for over twenty-five years. The term 'Paki-bashing' was coined in 1969 on the Collingwood Estate in Bethnal Green. Since then racial attacks and harassment, particularly against Asian people, have increased considerably, and certain London boroughs, particularly Tower Hamlets, Camden and Newham, have figured prominently in the increase. It took many years and great effort to convince the police of the seriousness of the problem. Racial harassment today is much more widespread than most authorities admit, and it may take years for some agencies to recognise, or admit, the problem.

Research also shows that the treatment of black people within the criminal justice system reveals serious levels of discrimination. Prejudice and the manifestation of racism within the police force has long been a focus of concern, and it is only recently that the issues have begun to be taken seriously within the force. Even now the degree of self-criticism and self-scrutiny within the Metropolitan Police leaves much to be desired. Nor is the Church's record very good in relating to the police with a healthy suspicion and scrutiny. Chaplaincy work, and secret meetings between senior police and bishops, are a woefully inadequate approach to so serious an area involving accountability and public debate.

THE POLITICS OF RACE AND THE RESURGENCE OF FASCISM

The decade of the 1970s was marked by the rise of various fascist groups, often appealing to disillusioned former supporters of 'mainstream' parties and discontented elements within local communities. Thus substantial sections of the white working class in the East End formed the social base for the National Front in the late 1970s. 'The social base of the NF,' claimed Martin Webster, a fascist leader of the time, in 1979, 'is made up of the desperate and dispossessed among the white working class.' Most of these came from former Labour voters, but there was also a large group of deeply alienated youth, some of whom were too young to vote but who found in the NF an identity and a community. Since then groups such as the NF have fragmented, while the racist elements within the Conservative Party and the tabloid press have become more explicit. Racism is now more respectable and acceptable than it has been for many years. Developments in Europe and Hong Kong as well as at home have brought to the surface some of the more unpleasant facets of racism and xenophobia in Britain as elsewhere in Europe where facism and anti-semitism are on the increase.

The appeal of fascism to the young should be a matter of great importance to the churches for that appeal is often of a quasi-religious kind. While other parties offer better social and economic prospects, and shops and stores taunt with competing types of consumer goods, the fascist movement offers risk, danger and challenge, and the excitement and thrill of being part of a crusade. In 1958 the novelist Colin MacInnes warned that there was 'the raw material of crypto-fascism of the worst kind' within the contemporary youth culture. He had in mind the Teddy Boys of the late

1950s, about whom he wrote in his novel *Absolute Beginners* (1958), and he did not believe that a fascist movement was very likely. Today the position is more serious. There has recently been much attention in the international media to the rise of 'Neo-Nazism' in Germany. Less attention has been given to the growth of Nazism among British youth, a revival which goes back some years beyond the German equivalent. In a 1983 study of fifth formers (15–16 year olds) in east London, 14 per cent said that the National Front or the British Movement was their first choice of political party, and a further 16 per cent saw them as their second choice. Few of them knew much about the parties except that they were anti-black. The 1980s saw both the disintegration and fragmentation of the far right parties and the growth of racist positions over a wider area. At the same time, while the fascist parties themselves were in disarray, their base of support had widened. A 1987 study reported: 'In 1979 support for the fascist parties was confined to a hard core of male skinheads who were deliberately seeking a violent form of rebellion. By 1982 support was coming from a wider section.' During the 1980s it was widely believed that the electoral prospects of the fascist parties had declined beyond recovery, and that the real danger was that of a shift to physical violence. But in 1993 this view received a dramatic jolt.

THE ISLE OF DOGS
At a by-election in September 1993 voters in Millwall on the Isle of Dogs elected the fascist (BNP) councillor Derek Beackon. There had been BNP activity on the island for some time, exploiting deep resentments about housing. In the by-election of October 1992 the BNP candidate Barry Osborne obtained 20 per cent of the poll (657 votes), the highest fascist vote for over a decade. There is no doubt that there is a lot of racism in the area, though always preceded by 'I'm not racist but . . .'. Most people know in broad terms what the BNP stands for, and so know what

they are doing. On the other hand, we have heard all kinds of reasons why people voted BNP ('I voted BNP because they're going to keep the school bus,' said one resident) and why people didn't vote at all. The atmosphere just before and during the election, with large numbers of thugs imported from Essex, Hertfordshire, Croydon and elsewhere, was extremely intimidating. The commonest explanation was that it was 'a protest vote', an expression of anger, against a Tory Government, a Liberal Democrat Council, and a Labour neighbourhood which people felt had failed them.

There were and are deeper issues: in particular, the climate created by the Canary Wharf development, and the growth of a small and isolated Bengali community. The period of BNP activity coincided almost exactly with the life of the London Docklands Development Corporation (LDDC), set up in 1981. This development has made the Isle of Dogs known throughout the world, but it has done little to improve conditions for local people, black or white. The persistence of unemployment, poor housing and a general sense of neglect has provided fertile ground for racist explanations. Unemployment in Docklands is almost as high as it was in 1981 and in some places it is higher. Most of the new jobs have not gone to local residents. In 1989 twelve of the biggest office firms in the Isle of Dogs reported that only 3 per cent of their workforce lived locally. For local people the development has meant noise, dust and dirt, roads driven through their estate, increased illness, and mounting resentment at the contrast with the gentrification nearby.

A report by Docklands Forum, a local monitoring unit, showed the failure of the local authority to stand by a housing-allocations policy based on need. It discussed the crucial role of Masthouse Terrace, the only social housing scheme built since 1981, and the way in which rumours of preferential treatment for Bengalis fuelled the recent campaign. The loss of council housing and the failure to develop a social housing policy are at the heart of the present crisis.

The provision of social housing must be 'the benchmark against which to judge the Corporation's record', wrote Robert Key MP from the Department of the Environment in 1991. But 78 per cent of the new housing in Docklands is private, much of it at the luxury end of the market. Seventy-five per cent of those who have bought houses in Docklands have incomes over £10,000 per annum, but less than 2 per cent of local residents earn this amount. There has been no new council housing for more than ten years. As the Association of Island Communities observed, 'The ground is being laid for social polarisation and conflict.'

It was into this tense atmosphere that a small Bengali community, around 11 per cent of the population, came. It is a very small proportion of the East End's Bengalis who live, or want to live, in the Isle of Dogs. Since they have arrived, they have been subjected to racial harassment and attacks, and these have increased throughout the Island and the adjacent Poplar area. In 1987–8, 104 attacks were reported in the Isle of Dogs (at a time when only 260 Bengali families lived there). In 1988–9 the figure was 202. In 1992, 475 racial incidents (including attacks, graffiti, insults and threats) were reported in Tower Hamlets as a whole, and this grew to 565 in 1993. Tower Hamlets accounts for 6.3 per cent of all reported racial incidents in England and Wales, and these figures are certainly an under-statement of the true position. It was the attack on Quddus Ali in September 1993 in Commercial Road, midway between the main Bengali area and the Isle of Dogs, which sparked off the recent wave of protests.

As Ruth Glass showed in her study of North Kensington in 1960, it is not the simple existence of prejudice and intolerance which creates social conflict, but the absence or weakness of positive forces working in the opposite direction. It is where tolerance is timid that prejudice is infectious. So the role of publicly identified groups and individuals in shaping and shifting a climate of thought and behaviour is crucial. The most tragic feature of recent East End life has been the collapse of any progressive political vision. Politics became no more than civil war carried on by other means. The area has been poorly served by its politicians, particularly from the mid 1980s when a new type of 'Liberal' emerged, lacking the depth and vision of an earlier generation, more populist and narrow. In spite of the denials, some of them seemed to hold views similar to those expressed by the BNP. Faced with Labour and Liberals who equivocated and used euphemisms, and the BNP who said clearly what they meant, people who wanted 'rights for whites' chose the latter.

Yet I believe that some good has come from this sordid vote. Already there is clear evidence of a new radicalisation among Bengali youth. Youth Connections, a federation of Bengali youth, has brought together large numbers of previously 'unpoliticised' young Bengalis. The work done by Sue Mayo, appointed as support worker by the churches on the Isle of Dogs from September 1993 to May 1994, helped to change the climate of opinion, and certainly contributed to the very high poll which defeated the BNP at the May elections. If it has taken the election of a fascist to bring about a new sense of unity and solidarity, a sense of the need for renewed multi-racial politics, the future could be exciting and hopeful. Yet there is still a lot of work to be done if we are to forge inter-racial networks of co-operation at the local level.

RELIGION AND CHANGE IN LONDON

Afro-Caribbean and Asian communities contain very large and vigorous religious traditions, including Christian, Muslim, Hindu, Sikh and others. The bulk of Christians of Afro-Caribbean origin are now outside the 'mainstream' churches, in contrast to the situation in the Caribbean before mass immigration. The growth of the black-led (mainly

Pentecostal) churches is a post-racism phenomenon, a response to the negative experience of black Christians in the 'mainstream' churches. In many inner-city districts black-led churches constitute the bulk of the Christian presence. Many of them are heavily influenced by the otherworldly spirituality which has been inherited from the USA, while the more radical and prophetic dimension of the black liberation tradition has not affected them. But this is changing. There is a growing body of dissent and discontent with the reduced gospel of the pietists, and we may expect to see a growth of more radical elements among black Christians in the coming years.

Yet it is the churches' contact with Asian people of other faith traditions which constitutes the major problem area for the next decade. The growth of Islam in London has been one of the most striking social and cultural shifts of recent years, and there are now more practising Muslims in Tower Hamlets than practising Christians. Many people express concern about 'Muslim fundamentalism' and its appeal to deprived Asian youth. Yet Asian youth are affected by many forces, and many have succumbed to the worst features of western secularism. The culture of Islam is as open to change and development as is any faith tradition, and there is an urgent need for Christians and Muslims to build bridges and work together, recognising the differences but seeking the common ground. In particular it is important that the progressive forces within the different faith traditions learn to work together, and resist the potential for the growth of bigotry and intolerance. For intolerance is never so dangerous as when it assumes a religious form.

THE CHALLENGE FOR THE CHRISTIAN COMMUNITY

The issue of racism has not been engaged theologically or as a central gospel imperative by the church leaderships in London until recently, and even now only partially. In the immediate post-war period there was some marginal church activity among black communities in the East End and elsewhere, but for the most part black people were ignored by the churches. The inability of the churches in Notting Hill to respond to the situation at the time of the 1958 riots is well known, and it contributed to the wider alienation of black Christians from the white-led churches. Since those days there has undoubtedly been a growing consciousness and growing action in relation to racism by Christian groups, black and white. Yet experience in a multi-racial society or an evangelical commitment to rooting out this 'erroneous and strange doctrine' of racism does not seem to have played a significant role in the appointment of bishops and church leaders. (In the Church of England, attitudes to the ordination of women seem to have been more important in appointing bishops to multi-racial areas than their understanding and experience of, or attitude to, racism.) Yet racism goes deep within the Christian community itself. Churches are far better at attacking sleazy and sordid groups of back-street thugs uttering racist slogans than at combating the reputable racism of those who smile, speak well and are charming, and most likely are church members.

One of the real weaknesses of the Church in its response to race matters has been the tendency to see race as an appendage, a special interest area. So, just as we have appointed chaplains to industry, universities, hospitals and prisons, so we have appointed chaplains to black people. 'Chaplaincy' work will undoubtedly continue, and many of the chaplains are good and holy people, but it is a patronising and racist model of action. The future lies with prophecy, not chaplaincy, and with the recognition that the struggle against racism has to occur at the heart of the gospel and the heart of the structures of the Church, not on the margins. Racism threatens Christian faith at its very foundations: it threatens the renunciation and the covenant made at baptism, as it threatens the equality and sharing of life in the Eucharist. It needs to be attacked here at the very heart of Christian worship and practice. Racism is like a barium meal which reveals other inequalities, injustices and disorders within the organism. Or, to change the metaphor, for the Church to engage with racism seriously is to open a Pandora's box of unfinished theological and spiritual business.

The Christian community has taken racism into its system. Its collusion with racism is part and parcel of a deeper and more pervasive collusion with the false values of the world. If there is to be a powerful and consistent resistance to racism by the Church in London, there must be a massive disaffiliation from the dominant structures and a return to gospel values and the liberating message of Jesus. It is a choice between life and death. We must choose life.

Part II

•

ADDRESSING THE SITUATION

Chapter Five

RESPONDING TO DRUG USERS

●

ADELE BLAKEBROUGH[*]

When Eric Blakebrough accepted the call to become the minister of the John Bunyan Baptist Church in 1967, he came to a church, nearly one hundred years old, with a declining membership. The church which had once flourished in a residential area was now on a traffic island in the midst of a one-way system, the railway and Kingston's rapidly growing shopping centre. He came, passionately believing that the local church must have a vision of God's will being worked out in its neighbourhood. The members of the church shared this belief but were at a loss to know what its neighbourhood was and how best to serve it.

Eric and Mary, his wife, spent some weeks trying to understand and assess the needs of the local community. It was soon obvious that large numbers of young people congregated two hundred yards from the church, near the railway station. Here a semi-circle of pubs reflected the interest of the youth groups. The Three Fishes was packed with hippies, listening to the powerful music of Pink Floyd, Led Zeppelin and the Rolling Stones, who at one time rehearsed at Kingston. Many were in the dream world of hallucinogenic drugs. Opposite was the Kingston Hotel, venue for the 'Skinhead' group. Completing the triangle was the South Western public house, playing heavy rock music

[*] © Adele Blakebrough 1995

and favoured by the Hell's Angels. Further afield was The Swan which catered for the 'Teddy Boys'; the Mods were accommodated in another pub nearby. When the bell rang in the pubs at 11 pm, the groups would make their way to the railway and bus stations. Clashes were inevitable and especially noticeable on Friday nights when most of the young people were reluctant to go home anyway.

This was part of our community – volatile, at odds with each other and with the adult community. Apart from Carwardine's Coffee Shop, also a popular venue in the day, and the pubs, there seemed to be no other acceptable social place. State youth clubs and uniformed organisations had no appeal for these young people. Also, growing like mushrooms overnight, squats were formed in empty houses and were attractive to youngsters who felt alienated from their families. Another magnet for those who sought to live in community without rules or regulation, or who wanted to realise the dream of life lived in peace and love with the freedom to experiment with drugs, was the defunct hotel on Eel Pie island.

So this became the immediate and urgent task of the church, to serve young people. The idea emerged of providing a safe but acceptable club on a Friday night where these youngsters could meet together. In order to protect those vulnerable ones who would be out all night and to provide an alternative to the squats where there was pressure to have sex and take drugs, and where there was often violence and theft, it was decided that the Friday Night Club must open from 10 pm to 6 am. One of the church halls was transformed, by means of loans from church members, into a sophisticated area, with lowered ceilings, orange and purple walls, a well-equipped bar for food, coffee and soft drinks. A good hi-fi system was essential. No alcohol was to be served. The name 'Kaleidoscope' was suggested, the concept being that each piece of coloured glass in a kaleidoscope is not significant in itself, but brought together with others makes a beautiful pattern.

This was the dream, to bring all these people together in one club where there would be harmony, a wonderful variety of life experience and shared hopes: The Banquet of the Kingdom of God, where everyone sits down together regardless of class, status or culture!

Churches are often naive enough to take on the impossible task. At first all that happened was that all the fights and confrontations were transferred to the Kaleidoscope Club. However, the church clung stubbornly to its vision that every human being is accepted by God. By persistence, and more important, by the intervention of three young hippies who became persuaded of the Christian faith and joined the church, the club decor was changed, the food became vegetarian, the music less loud and aggressive and the club became the most popular young people's venue in Kingston-upon-Thames.

It soon became apparent that to provide a good social place was not enough. Many of the young people who used the club were suffering from drug abuse and illnesses related to poor accommodation, malnutrition, pregnancy and self-neglect. Those who were homeless did not have a GP. The next challenge was to provide a medical service for those in need on a Friday night. How could this be achieved?

A large Sunday School cupboard, measuring 8ft by 6ft, which opened off from the club was emptied, wallpapered, carpeted and two comfortable chairs installed. A local GP, funded by a generous benefactor, was employed to be available to our customers from 10 pm to 2 am every Friday. So began the medical work of the club.

It also became apparent that other young people were homeless or living in terrible conditions, so the caretaker's house next to the church was turned into a makeshift hostel. Jan Johnston, one of the three hippy friends, was put in charge. Again, it was imperative to learn and adapt to new situations. The house was not ideal: those living in the downstairs rooms opened the sash windows at night and admitted their friends. Eric, passing someone on the stairs one night, asked, 'Who are you?' The response was, 'Well, who are you?'

As the club became increasingly popular and the hostel often full with youngsters who had run away from home or from the care of the local authority, the community reacted against the work of the church. Drug-taking and caring for drug users was, and still is, an emotive issue. The police raided the Friday Club one Friday in 1974. The doctor was asked to leave, the nurse was strip-searched and ordered to hand over the medical records. She refused, but the police took a file with about ninety names. As a result of protests and the arrival of a local magistrate known to us the file was not taken, but the police demanded the names, which were read out to them. It is assumed that the police thought that they were garnering a comprehensive list of local drug offenders. The next day a local newspaper led with the headline, 'Police raid Club after five found dead'. The headline referred to police evidence that five young people in Kingston had overdosed and died over a period of two years.

The church members and staff of the project were dismayed and shocked, but also had an overwhelming sense of the injustice done to our clients and to the project. During the weeks that followed powerful allies emerged. *The Guardian* newspaper took up the issue, as did the Royal College of Nurses and the National Council of Civil Liberties, and a benefactor paid for the services of the well-known Queen's Council, Mr Louis Blom-Cooper, to be at our disposal. The local community had to 'take sides' and soon officers from the town's Youth Service and the Social Services spoke out on Kaleidoscope's behalf.

There was a 'sea change' in the feelings of the young people towards the club and those who worked there. Even the Hell's Angels, who were volatile members of the club, gave their allegiance. It was acknowledged by all those who used the club that the workers and church were 'in trouble' and yet they stood with them and identified with them, and even more, were advocates for them. From that time onwards the club had a united feeling; a tradition of loyalty and mutual respect became established and this particular community 'drew together'.

It became apparent that the church buildings, the church halls and the caretaker's house were inadequate to meet the needs of both the church itself and those using Kaleidoscope. The Victorian church, with its 700 seats, 12 ft high pulpit, galleries and adjacent halls, was falling into a bad state of repair. The membership had risen from thirty-five to sixty, but the church was far too big and unlikely to be filled again. The central heating broke down, the toilets rarely functioned properly; the decoration and repairs needed both to the church buildings and to the caretaker's house were beyond our financial ability to meet.

A brave and bold decision needed to be made about the future. At an historic church meeting in 1970 it was the decision of the majority of church members that the church buildings should be demolished and that a new, purpose-built complex should be erected on the site. This would include a smaller church, seating 200, a prayer chapel, the club, a community hall, a hostel, an office and medical facilities. So began a new dream which had to be realised through hard work, perseverance and the overcoming of countless difficulties.

Eric worked closely with the architect, David Cole, to design buildings which would create the right environment where people would feel 'at home' and where function would be allied with flair. The church itself is based on the Protestant Church in Plotzensee, Berlin, which is in a square formation with the communion table in the middle. The design is simple, in brick with a honeycombed concrete ceiling, with stained-glass windows by John Hayward and added treasures as the years have gone by: a ceramic flight of angels created by Victor Bryant, paintings by Myfanwy Franks, an iron crown of thorns over the communion table, donated by Alan and Uschi Roberts, an offertory table made by the boys in our carpentry workshop and many other gifts. The central communion table, made by Richard Fitzsimmonds expresses the centrality of the Eucharist in the worship of the church. A prayer chapel sited next to the church provides a quiet place to meditate and pray and is used daily for holy communion. Above the church, a community hall was built with wooden floors and ceilings and red-brick walls.

The Friday night club is situated in the basement of the church. This new design had to incorporate features of the old club, a place not brightly lit, with shadowy corners and a sense of security. Eventually a design was agreed; dark green walls, slate-coloured floor tiles, brick and concrete, dark furniture, lamps that looked like gas lamps lit by the soft light of carbon filament bulbs. But, most important, the bar at the end of the room had to symbolise 'homecoming'. There is a long wooden counter, behind which glows a large red Aga cooker, a Welsh dresser loaded with decorative plates, and a red Gaggia coffee machine. There is the smell of homemade bread and food. There are pottery cups and plates, never plastic! Off the club area are two surgeries giving easy access to medical facilities.

The four-storey hostel, across the courtyard from the church, resembles a red-brick fortress – a place of safety and asylum for young people who have been hurt. David Cole was given the task of designing four flats where each room had a different shape and which were grouped round a sitting room with a real fireplace, expressing the theme of homecoming.

Next came the task of raising the money needed. £500,000 was the estimated cost. The Kaleidoscope (Kingston) Housing Association was formed to enable us to borrow £300,000 from the Department of the Environment, which sum was to be paid back in rents. The Department of Education and Science made a grant of £18,000, the local authority gave £9,000, land needed for road widening gave us another £30,000, there was a bequest for £23,000, and the church sold its manse on the understanding that our family would move into the new hostel. Endless fundraising events were organised and somehow the necessary money was raised. Planning permission, however, took six years to obtain. The community and local authority were cautious about these new plans. It took intense lobbying of councillors, innumerable speeches at public meetings, letters to the press, discussions and debate to obtain the final permission. Those years were hard and tried everyone's faith. How long could we go on? Were we really being led forward by the Spirit into this new phase?

Eventually the longed-for day dawned – the day of the official opening of the new buildings. Lord Tonypandy, then George Thomas MP, Speaker of the House of Commons, conducted the official opening, and the Reverend Dr Ernest Payne, Vice President of the Baptist Union and a past President of the World Council of Churches preached. Over a thousand people passed through the buildings that day; there was jubilation and thanksgiving. A new era had begun.

Mixed with this euphoria was some apprehension, however. There were questions in our minds. Would our clients still come to the club? How would the hostel work? Would enough money come in to pay the staff and the bills?

Within a few years it became apparent that we needed to appoint a psychiatrist to develop Kaleidoscope as a centre for the treatment of drug dependants. It had to be someone who agreed with our idea of bringing the hospital to the clients, to base the treatment in the community, to allow a 'low threshold' for those coming for treatment, to accept people as they are – in other words, to establish a client-centred service. Dr Shanmuganathan fitted our criteria and his views reflected the community-based approach. He was appointed in 1980 and has since obtained a Diploma in Addictive Behaviour. His gentle, kind manner and the way he has always shown respect for our clients has endeared him to clients and staff alike. Under his leadership the medical service has expanded and deepened in quality.

The club soon became a popular venue again. A wonderful mixture of people poured in on Friday nights – students, 'way-out' people, bikers, the lonely, the mentally ill, taxi drivers and bus drivers on their way home, a rich diversity of people enjoying the ambience, the welcoming smiles of the staff and the food. The surgeries became so busy that two more nurses had to be appointed, as well as a new, part-time, doctor to assist Dr Shanmuganathan. Dr David Marjot has been our consultant psychiatrist through this period and has recently held daytime clinics at Kaleidoscope.

The hostel was soon filled with young people who referred themselves or who were referred by Social Services as being in need of care and long-term rehabilitation. Because many of those who joined the staff were from other denominations, and in particular from the Roman Catholic tradition, a liturgy was devised that enabled most people to participate and worship in our Baptist fellowship. The church was becoming truly ecumenical. In 1980, Sister Frances Makower of the Society of the Sacred Heart, joined the staff team and became an associate member of our church.

Challenges came apace and there was little breathing space to stand back and contemplate. We daily dispensed methadone as a substitute for heroin. As word spread that we could be trusted and that we had a 'no appointments' clinic every Wednesday and that it often took no longer than two days to be admitted on to the programme, more and more people came forward asking for help.

As the numbers who came to us for treatment increased, there became an urgent need to give them advice or social support and opportunities to build confidence and create real possibilities. We bought the two houses next to our complex; one became the manse, the other the tutor's house, with welcoming rooms, lined with books and equipped with computers. A fine art workshop was built in the garden. Another area was needed to provide cheap, nourishing food during the day, so the laundry in the hostel was resited and the basement room became the coffee bar. Firms, trusts, churches and individuals were persuaded to contribute towards these new ventures. Meanwhile the surgeries were under great pressure to meet the needs of all those seeking help.

In 1986, the Kaleidoscope Project began a needle exchange to limit the risk of HIV and hepatitis infections resulting from the use of dirty needles. We were one of the first organisations in the UK to implement this exchange. Some people were critical of this approach, but we do not want to be judgemental and the reality is that people use this facility every day. We opened a twenty-four-hour help line, staffed by people, not an answerphone. Parents, friends and users need the emotional support of a human voice at the end of a telephone when they want to speak to someone urgently. Staff are trained to answer appropriately and to refer to appropriate members of the team anyone who calls with anxieties or specific needs. All these initiatives, including a training bakery, needed financial support. It has, thankfully, been our experience that funding from various sources eventually comes and we have not seriously had to reduce our work through funding problems, but the struggle is constant.

In 1986 the Department of Education launched a nationwide programme of drug education, mainly to be executed by teachers. Kingston Borough Council, which was familiar with Kaleidoscope's work in the town, asked the project to contract to provide the service. Sally Murray, a qualified social worker, who had worked with youngsters on the Doddington Estate in an Intermediate Treatment programme and who was a long-term volunteer at Kaleidoscope, was appointed to run this new department. The Education Department met 70 per cent of the cost for a three-year period. The first step was to train a network of teachers, educational welfare officers, school nurses, health visitors, youth leaders, social workers and police officers. Ten individuals a month attended a one-week course at

Kaleidoscope, which covered subjects from the pharmacology of drugs to the social characteristics of drug users.

By listening to thousands of drug users telling him their life stories, Eric had isolated five basic criteria for spotting potential drug-abuse problems. The result is that Kaleidoscope built up a remarkable network of contacts at all levels of the education and caring professions in the town. By the end of the three-year funding period, we had three teachers in each secondary school in the area, trained to identify young people at risk of drug misuse and familiar with Kaleidoscope and its staff. Primary schools were also involved. Our team went into schools; children were referred for counselling at Kaleidoscope; in some cases it was decided that a hostel place would be appropriate.

When funding ceased we had to continue this work using our own charity-funded core resources, with the help of a small grant from Social Services of £1,000 a year. There was never a question of giving up the important work of preventive and interventional strategies with children. It has caused extra headaches for the fundraising team and called for imaginative approaches by the Training Unit, but the work goes on and in fact is extending its scope to encompass professionals from overseas, theological colleges and church workers.

The most serious obstacle has been, surprisingly, the new government reform, as published in the White Paper in January 1989 'Working for Patients'. The reforms were intended to extend patient choice, to delegate responsibility to those best placed to respond to patients' needs and to secure the best value for money. We saw this as a new and exciting challenge we were keen to accept. This provision should allow all those who choose to have treatment at Kaleidoscope to be able to do so under the National Health Service.

The reality is very different. The 'free market' has not generally benefited the voluntary sector; in fact, most voluntary agencies have experienced greater difficulties. In the drug-agency field problems were foreseen and representations were made to the Government that money allocated to drug services should be 'ring-fenced'. It was argued that health and local authorities should be held accountable for channelling funds to voluntary drug agencies. The Government refused to do this, with predictable results.

There has been inadequate separation between purchaser and providers. Not surprisingly, consultants who advise the NHS managers about awarding contracts give highest priority to securing hospital services. The voluntary sector has been in a weak position to negotiate contracts. Suddenly it seemed that all our clients were at risk. We had made a commitment to them which might not prove to be financially viable. After a period of acute anxiety, our local health authority formed a purchasing consortium of local district health authorities to pay for medical services provided by Kaleidoscope. The relief we felt was palpable. But six months into the financial year, Merton and Sutton Health Authority indicated that they had not ratified the contract and would not pay for the treatment of patients resident in their district who had received treatment at Kaleidoscope. The sum involved was about £95,000. Then there began a campaign to discredit Kaleidoscope. The Merton and Sutton Health Authority wrote letters 'in confidence' undermining the credibility of Kaleidoscope. We took legal advice and were told that we had a strong case but the cost of legal action would be too high for a voluntary organisation to meet.

In church meetings and staff meetings we agonised over the problem. Did we have to let these people go? Could we break the relationship we had built up with them over a long period of time? Were they to be denied choice of treatment? In the event we could not reject them and we settled in to a long campaign. We canvassed churches, organisations and individuals to support us financially to keep these people in treatment whilst we fought for their right to choose. My father had hoped that when he resigned from being Director at the end of 1992 these conflicts with Merton and Sutton Health Authority would have been resolved. This was not to be and the negotiations continue.

In 1993 the NHS Health Advisory Service made an inspection of Kaleidoscope. A team of four inspectors examined every aspect of the service we provide for 'Problem Drug Misusers'. In their Draft Report, which we have seen, it is noted that the Kaleidoscope 'is required to provide a level of information about its activities which far exceeds that required by the statutory services'. The inspectors draw attention to the difficulties we have experienced with Merton and Sutton Health Authority with regard to contracts. Referring to the proposal that clients should be redirected back to Merton and Sutton, the inspectors state: 'This policy runs counter not only to Kaleidoscope's open access policy, but also to Advisory Council on the Misuse of Drugs recommendations and Patients' Charter guidelines.' Turning to the services we provide, the report states: 'We were impressed by the quality of care offered to clients individually and as a group.' Further, the report says: 'The level of uptake of Kaleidoscope's service indicates positive customer choice and a high degree of satisfaction with the service. It is highly accessible and operates two evening medical surgeries for which no appointment is necessary.'

In the last section of their report, the inspectors highlight commendable features in the provision of services to Problem Drug Misusers. The team give their highest commendation, 'Good in the National Context', to Kaleidoscope, with the comment: '... the integration of social care facilities with a tightly controlled, but easily accessible methadone programme which is provided by Kaleidoscope. We are aware of no comparable service within the UK.' I quote this from this official report because it contradicts attacks made on us by some of our opponents.

I had been appointed to the pastorate of the John Bunyan Baptist Church in 1984 and acted as Assistant to the Director, becoming familiar with the management of the project and negotiations with statutory bodies. On 1st January 1993 I was appointed Director. Eric and Mary moved to Wales and Eric remained Chairman of the management committees. In spite of ongoing problems with statutory bodies I was taking office in an exciting time for the project. I had seen it grow from small beginnings to a project recognised nationally and internationally for its innovative work with drug dependants and marginalised young people. I knew that the increased numbers of staff and the complexity of our work made a review of our management structure my first priority.

A year before I became Director we had secured a large site adjoining our present buildings. Our hope was to provide a hostel for those of our clients who had become ill with HIV/AIDS, to support those who were suffering from drug-related illness, and to give asylum to those who have reached 'the end of their tether' and cannot cope with their situation. In addition we planned to provide a covered area for the fifty or sixty of our clients who come daily for support. Most of them lead chaotic lives and seek the security and supervised social interaction that we have so far been able to offer only in the courtyard area; the coffee bar can accommodate only twenty at a time. A larger medical reception area and a bigger and better coffee bar were incorporated into the design. A house, to provide better accommodation for the training courses and to supply residential accommodation for the increasing numbers of visitors from abroad, completed the plan, with gardens linking the whole.

In 1994 we submitted the plans to the council for planning permission. We had been aware for some time that the presence of some of our clients made the residents in the road anxious. None of them had ever abused, threatened or attacked anyone in the street, but a group of loud-voiced people, sometimes arguing amongst themselves and often distressed, are perceived to be a threat, although our relationship with them in the open courtyard was positive and gave them a safe area to be in. The police have been very helpful. We hold regular residents' meetings to listen to the views of local people and explain what we are trying to do. It is an unfortunate fact that most people do not want to see or be made aware of drug dependency. It is of little consolation to those living near us that the majority of dependants who come to us for treatment would hardly be noticed. The clinic is open from 7 am to 11 pm and many of those who work come early, or later in the evening; they are like any other citizens, working in offices, shops and public institutions. They have families and live 'normal' lives. However, 20 per cent of our clients are in a state of turmoil, they are often homeless, suffer broken relationships, or have experienced serious abuse of all kinds. It is this group we are anxious to serve better than we can at present.

The planning permission and a subsequent appeal were turned down chiefly on the grounds that we did not have planning permission to operate a day centre and it was not thought suitable to locate such a facility in Cromwell Road, which is in a residential area, even if it is the main relief road taking traffic out of Kingston. It was anticipated that such a development would create noise and disturbance and problems of on-street parking. We are of course disappointed that we cannot enhance the quality of some of our clients' lives in the way that we envisaged. However, it is 'back to the drawing board' to devise another plan. We also realise we have much work to do to inform and encourage our community to accept people who are hurt and who feel isolated, within the borough we all live in.

We have recently started work with the children of drug dependants. We have been anxious about these children for some time. They were part of a volatile group of clients, witnesses to many disturbing scenes, and, although loved by their parents, they often received too little or too much attention. On a recent visit to Kaleidoscope Dr Helmut Sell of the World Health Organisation made the observation that these children were like street children the world over and needed a secure and stable environment in which to learn to play and use their imaginative skills. Shortly afterwards, Mary returned from a conference in America where she had been impressed by an experiment amongst the same kind of parents and children we are working with. A playgroup had been established in a hall, which was brightly decorated and had kitchen facilities. There was a well-equipped 'play house' and a 'clothes corner' for the exchange of children's clothes and shoes. Outings, a magazine, parties and discussions all helped to make a happy, positive atmosphere where the difficult task of parenting was shared by others.

Determined to implement some of this valuable work, Kaleidoscope, through the generous support of the Linbury Trust, appointed two workers in September 1992. The hall was equipped and, with the help of another charity, a two-storey model house with kitchen, dining room, bedroom and small 'garden' was constructed. It is much loved and used by the children. A Christmas party organised by the parents was an outstanding success and twenty children are now on the register.

Kaleidoscope has attracted the interest of those working in the drug field in Asia and countries in Eastern Europe. Community-based centres are more economical to run than expensive hospital services. After Eric visited Nepal in 1989, a club similar to Kaleidoscope was established in Kathmandu and is run by Nepalese staff. Uli Kohler has been appointed as our Development Officer, responsible for making contacts in Europe and Asia, arranging visits to Kaleidoscope, organising conferences and seminars. His network of contacts has already led to visits to Kaleidoscope by professionals in the drug field from Nepal, India, Africa, South-east Asia, Poland, Bulgaria, Romania, France, Germany and other European countries. He organised two conferences in 1994, led by members of staff in Russia and Bulgaria. In June 1994 Kaleidoscope hosted a European Consultation for professionals considering community-based drug projects.

The challenges ahead are many. I am aware of all the pressures on staff and volunteers to continue to give quality service. It is hard to be patient and hopeful in the face of legislation which seems designed to marginalise even more those who are already marginalised. However, I remind myself of the words with which Eric concluded his book *No Quick Fix*, 'Statutory services carry out statutory provisions. The Church, seeking to love God and humanity, must carry out deeds of love. That is the nature of the Church. God is love. The Kingdom of God is where love reigns. Kaleidoscope is not the Kingdom of God. But it strives to build that Kingdom in one small part of London.'[1]

---

[1] Eric Blakebrough, *No Quick Fix*, Marshall Pickering, 1986.

Chapter Six

HELPING THE HOMELESS*

●

SISTER BRIDIE DOWD

Long before Westminster Cathedral was built, the Daughters of Charity of St Vincent de Paul, welcomed by Cardinal Manning, were engaged in work with the poor in the Westminster area. Sister Catherine Chatelaine, a French woman, and an Irish Sister moved from York Street to Carlisle Place in 1863. Their friends, Lady Georgina and her companions, decided to buy the land on which the first part of the house was to be built. They raised the money by means of a great bazaar, as they wanted to hand the house over to the sisters without debt. For some unknown reason the money was never used for this purpose. Sister Chatelaine found herself in a large, unfinished house with a debt of £6,000. This meant that she had to raise the sum of £300 a year for thirty-five years, quarter by quarter. How she managed it is little short of a miracle.

While money was very scarce, orphan children were very plentiful. Cardinal Manning wanted Catholic children to be withdrawn from the workhouse and cared for in Catholic orphanages. Carlisle Place soon became the home of sixty children and forty babies, but there was no fixed or steady income to care for most of the children. There was also a night school for men and boys between the ages of twelve and forty. By 1877 the number of orphans had increased,

* © Sister Bridie Dowd 1995

so a new wing was built on the house, at a cost of £10,108. As work increased so the number of sisters grew.

In 1910 a further wing was built in order to provide more space for the children. Then in 1914 a need for a play area led to the development of the roof playground. In 1920 attics were raised to provide a Day Continuation School for girls over fourteen years. This work continued, with various changes made as the need arose, until 1974, when the transfer of schools took place, leaving a large, empty house. It was soon put to good use.

There was a demand for hostel accommodation in the area and this was quickly taken up. The De Montfort Sisters were looking for premises to set up a school for children with special needs. They took over a substantial part of the building. The upper two floors were leased to a housing association for a peppercorn rent. In 1979 Crisis at Christmas established themselves at the house. In 1980 Cardinal Hume requested office space to plan the papal visit.

All this provides a summary of the history of Carlisle Place up to the 1980s and shows how Divine Providence has been guiding and guarding the developments. The rest of this chapter will describe the effect of the Church in action on the development of the work of The Passage.

The Passage Day Centre and Nightshelter for Homeless People is situated in the heart of Westminster. It occupies a prominent position close to Westminster Cathedral, a five-minute walk away from Buckingham Palace and surrounded by the residences of the rich and the powerful. Its presence in this prime location gives it a unique position to proclaim and witness through its work to the Christian message:

> Take the case, my brothers, of someone who has never done a single good act but claims that he has faith. Will that faith save him? If one of the brothers or one of the sisters is in need of clothes and has not enough food to live on, and one of you says to them, 'I wish

you well; keep yourself warm and eat plenty', without giving them these bare necessities of life, then what good is that? Faith is like that: if good works do not go with it, it is quite dead.
(James 2:14–17)

The proximity of The Passage to the Victoria transport network – the trains, buses and coach stations which frequently provide temporary shelter for homeless people – is supremely advantageous for these people. When they are cold and hungry, alone and unwanted, The Passage is within easy reach for them. It is an oasis of hospitality, friendship, warmth and compassion in a city where these commodities are in short supply. The Passage operates under the umbrella of the St Vincent Centre and Westminster Cathedral – the Church in action.

The St Vincent Centre is managed and run by the Daughters of Charity of St Vincent de Paul. Vincent de Paul, their founder, was a French priest who ministered in various parishes in Paris in the early part of the seventeenth century. In many countries of the Western World he is a household name, renowned and honoured for his resourcefulness in caring for the poor and the refugees of his time. Following in his footsteps, the Daughters of Charity have, over the ensuing centuries, dedicated themselves to working tirelessly to lighten the burden of poverty and to dissipate its effects wherever it predominates. Vincent de Paul repeatedly reminded the women who formed the first communities of Daughters of Charity that they were daughters of God and daughters of the Church and that 'they were continuing the work that Jesus Christ had done while he was on earth'. That work is summed up in the well-known words of St Matthew's Gospel: 'When I was hungry, you gave me food, when I was thirsty you gave me a drink, when I was naked you clothed me. I was a stranger and you welcomed me.' And the reward is to 'enter into the joy of the Lord'. The 'option for the poor', about which so much is spoken in

Church circles in modern times, is practised daily by the administration, staff and volunteers of The Passage.

Until 1980 the clergy of Westminster Cathedral and the Daughters of St Vincent, independently of one another, had tried to relieve the hunger of the poor who knocked on their door by handing out packets of sandwiches. Realising that this was a short-term, inadequate measure and did not give much scope for pastoral care, the Sisters considered what more could be done. The only space available was a long wide corridor in the basement known as 'The Passage'. If that could be converted into use, it would provide a more humane way of giving sustenance to the hungry people who came daily to both doors. The space was there, the food would continue to come as it had done through the years, but what about furniture? By chance, one of the sisters noticed that a cafe nearby in Victoria Street wanted to dispose of its tables and chairs at a very low price, but collection had to be before 5 pm that day. There was no transport available, so Sister Eileen O'Mahoney, a tall, strong woman who was Superior and responsible for developments and would never let an opportunity pass her by, gathered a group of gentlemen around her and set off for the cafe. There was then seen a great procession of men carrying these heavy tables and chairs on their shoulders along Victoria Street. The furniture served well for many years!

Sister Eileen talked over the project with Father O'Donoghue, now Bishop O'Donoghue, and Anthony Bartlett, who lived locally and was a member of the St Vincent de Paul Society. Father O'Donoghue said that the Cathedral would be prepared to pay the salary of a person who would take responsibility for the day-to-day running. Sister Eileen knew a man who would be the right person to develop the project. Then it was asked what this venture should be called. Mr Bartlett suggested 'The Passage' for that is what it was and it could be a passage to a better way of life for many people.

The Passage was opened with a Mass celebrated there on a summer day in 1980. This mustard seed, a joint venture with Westminster Cathedral, from modest beginnings has developed in an unprecedented way – far beyond mere hospitality to the work of rehabilitation. A committee was formed, with Father O'Donoghue as Chairman and Anthony Bartlett as Vice Chairman.

The primary work of The Passage is the relief of poverty and the restoration of human dignity, as well as the improvement of life for the homeless. We operate an open-door policy which means that anyone can come to The Passage to seek help. Our prayer group, which is facilitated by Father Padraig Regan, a Vincentian Father, is the best attended weekly group meeting there: 'Not by bread alone can man live but on every word that comes from the mouth of God.'

The openness, strong faith, insight, forgiveness and reflectiveness seen there are striking. I call to mind a man of eighty-two who wanted an item of clothing. As the clothing store was closed he said he would go away and return later as there were people in the queue and if he stayed he would delay someone getting their dinner. Needless to say, he was taken to the clothing store there and then. His thoughtfulness and concern for others was impressive. It was while assisting him that we discovered he was sleeping in a doorway and that he had done so for a number of years since he lost his private accommodation.

In 1992 and 1993 major refurbishment took place and an extension was built so that we could give a better service. When this decision was reached the necessary funds were not available. As in 1863, when the Sisters first moved to Carlisle Place, we had to depend on Divine Providence. The work began in October 1992 and was completed in December 1993. We did not at any time keep the builders waiting for payment.

> So do not worry; do not say, "What are we to eat? What are we to drink? How are we to be clothed?" It is the pagans who set their hearts on all these things. Your

heavenly Father knows you need them all. Set your hearts on his kingdom first, and on his righteousness, and all these other things will be given you as well. So do not worry about tomorrow: tomorrow will take care of itself. Each day has enough trouble of its own.
(Matthew 6:31–34)

The trusts, companies, individuals – many of them anonymous – and the volunteers who have responded compassionately and generously to the needs of the centre and the people using it are an example of Christ's care for his loved ones. By their response they, too, are responding to Christ's call to all Christians to love our neighbour as ourselves. Here, in The Passage, preferential love is shown to the poor in practical terms, and their needs and rights are given the special attention which God has ordained for them. 'Poor' is understood in The Passage to refer to the economically disadvantaged who, as a consequence of their lack of status, suffer oppression and powerlessness. The manner in which these people are treated when they present themselves to seek help is the touchstone for the values that inform our thoughts, policies and actions, both of the management and all others engaged in the providing and caring services. It is central to the Christian faith we profess.

Bless those who persecute you: never curse them, bless them. Rejoice with those who rejoice and be sad with those in sorrow. Treat everyone with equal kindness; never be condescending but make real friends with the poor. Do not allow yourself to become self-satisfied.
(Romans 12:14–16)

The Passage, an example of Christian charity, evokes the words of a popular song of the 1960s: 'Have you seen the old girl who walks the streets of London, dirt in her hair, worn out shoes?' It is easy to fall into the trap of stereotyping the homeless people, as it is with any other group in the public eye. The media tends to focus on blameless, victimised youngsters or on elderly, alcoholic vagrants. While both images reflect realities, they do so only in part, for people are far more complex and defy such typecasting. So who are the homeless who come to our centre?

They could be anyone – you or me, given the same circumstances, which is a sobering thought. Homelessness can result from such circumstances as redundancy, prolonged unemployment, home repossession, a broken marriage or relationship, mental illness, personality disorders, institutional care from childhood, sexual and physical abuse and violence. Such experiences, if there is no support from family or friends, often lead people into alcoholism or drug abuse and a drift into crime and gambling. None of these things in isolation needs to lead to homelessness, but without the support of family or friends such experiences can be impossible to deal with single-handed. Homeless people come from all walks of life, social backgrounds and age groups.

An average of 300 people visit The Passage each day between the hours of 7 am and 2 pm. Basic needs are met. We provide cooked breakfasts and dinners, a warm place to sit in, clothing, showers and the use of a laundry. There is a medical service staffed by four volunteer nurses, with doctors from the Longmore Street general practice attending twice a week. A variety of treatment is provided for patients; this includes showering the infirm and mentally disturbed people (whose numbers seem to be increasing), treating those who are infested or suffering from scabies, dressing minor cuts and bruises, and caring for inflamed and blistered feet. We provide clean socks and shoes when these are available.

Women are in the minority and have a history of sleeping on the streets, though not out of choice. Some of the women have been harassed, threatened or abused at various times. Some are mentally ill and cannot cope alone. This also applies to a number of the men. They find a sense of acceptance and belonging, as well as friendship at The

Passage. Here they can think through their problems with staff, receive advice and obtain help. Practical matters such as washing clothes and obtaining new ones from the women's clothing store are important, as are the weekly cake and coffee mornings, and regular meals. In addition to meeting these basic needs, there is an equally important need we try to answer. This is the need to feel 'special', to be made a fuss of for a while, and to be valued for the unique human being that each one is. For those who are ready, the move towards rehabilitation is available. It is important to re-establish confidence and self-worth through relearning skills such as budgeting and shopping, through individual and group work, prayer and eventually resettlement into permanent accommodation.

In November 1990, at the sight of so many people sleeping on the Piazza at night in cardboard boxes, or wrapped in blankets, Cardinal Hume decided that something must be done. He arranged that the Cathedral Hall, in Ambrosden Avenue, would be used as a night shelter on a temporary basis, and he asked The Passage to find staff and volunteers. On the night of 9th December 1990, a team of four approached all those sleeping out in the immediate vicinity and took the names of those who were interested in coming the next night, and so it began! It was known as the Cathedral Night Shelter and it then took forty men and women off the streets every night and provided them with sleeping accommodation on mattresses on the floor. In July 1993 the Night Shelter was relocated from the Cathedral Hall to rented accommodation in Osbert Street, where there are now beds, washing facilities, showers and cooking facilities.

Both The Passage and the Night Shelter strive to treat all people with Christian compassion and respect. They continue to be run jointly with Westminster Cathedral. For all of us, whether in the direct or indirect service of people, compassion is the driving force; it motivates good caring, but of course one does not have to be a Christian to have compassion. Volunteers continue to be an integral part of The Passage and Night Shelter. They come and go, some for just an hour or two, giving valuable help before going to their daily jobs. Other volunteers trade in their lunch hour to lend a hand. Some even turn up on their days off. For others The Passage is their place of work. Ages range from twenty-one to well into the eighties, and people are from various ethnic backgrounds, all with a mutual purpose – the desire to be of service.

A fundamental aspect of the new life of the Church after Vatican II was the Church's attitude to the world. The Church is in the world which God created and upon which Jesus walked when he was on earth. In addition, new meaning and emphasis was given to the term 'the preferential love of the poor'. Until Vatican II, reason was the primary shaper of the Church's formulation of its social teaching. This teaching has gradually given way to the primacy of love, and love is the motivation to act on behalf of justice – justice for the marginalised, the despised and the down-and-out. It is love – the love that God has put into each heart for himself and for our neighbours – that inspires the devotion, compassion, generosity and hard work which are some of the integral components of the care and service daily provided by the staff and volunteers in The Passage. Reason could never achieve this.

The Church has always believed that Christ identifies with the poor and under-privileged. Now it looks at this truth in a new light with new urgency and new pastoral consequences. In reading the signs of the times, Christians see God's face above all in the face of suffering and wounded people. Fidelity to Christ requires that the people of God move from a passive role towards the poor to an active role. The shift is nowhere more obvious, more beneficial and more effective than in The Passage. Were it not for the very large numbers of generous, loving people imbued with the new understanding of their Christian obligations, coming forward to offer help of every kind, the setting up of The

Passage could never have happened. The volume of people in need and the extent of the problems which they present daily make very heavy demands on personnel and resources.

> You call me Master and Lord, and rightly; so I am. If I, then, the Lord and Master, have washed your feet, you should wash each other's feet. I have given you an example so that you may copy what I have done to you.
> (John 13:13-15).

The contribution of so many committed and devoted volunteers allows the specialist staff the facility to give as many people as much time as they need. The cost of this in financial terms would be exorbitant and therefore in many caring agencies unavailable. But it is precisely this very precious and expensive commodity, time, which enables and empowers people to take control of their own lives and this 'love in action' restores to them the independence and dignity which is their birthright.

> Being unemployed (and therefore poor) is to be in a fish bowl. You look out with demeaning, agonising envy at similar faces, the happy, normal, socially accepted people strolling through life with their spouses or lovers, getting into their posh cars, going to their middle class homes and their middle class pleasures; all hardly aware that they are virtually in paradise. In the affluent society, which worships wealth, poverty is spiritually painful. Nobody thanks you for being poor, and despite the Christian teaching on humility nobody thanks you for being a nobody. Eventually the Christian love affair with self-denial loses its charm. We all want to be wanted; but the unemployed are branded as unwanted; and every rejection by an employer nails you freshly to the cross of unwantedness. Unemployment is hell.'
> (From 'On The Dole', *The Tablet*, 19th February 1994)

As Christians we know and believe that women and men are created in the image and likeness of God. This entitles each and every one to a pre-eminent place in the social order, with inalienable rights, both political and socio-economic. The resources of the world must be equally shared by all. However, in real life things are not so simple. Until this dream becomes a reality there must be institutions like The Passage, where those of us who consider ourselves to be the 'haves' are given the opportunity to share what we have with the 'have nots'.

> I go to the poor to honour in their person the person of our Lord. I am going to see in them the incarnate wisdom of God.
>
> (Vincent de Paul)

Chapter Seven

CARING FOR PEOPLE WITH AIDS[*]

•

HELEN TAYLOR-THOMPSON

Monday, 14th December 1992 started as a dismal, dark and cold day. (The year happened to be the centenary of the building of Mildmay Mission Hospital on its present site.) As the afternoon wore on the weather deteriorated, yet, amidst the gloom, spirits were high at Mildmay: the reason was that part of the nurses' home in Austin Street was being demolished to make way for the new Family Care Centre, a unit for respite, rehabilitation and terminal care for families with AIDS – the first of its kind in the world.

But during the work human remains had been dug up; if they turned out to be more than 100 years old all work would have to stop, possibly for as long as six months. The experts came in and by the light of a small torch the bones were examined. Fortunately, I was able to enlighten them as to the history of Mildmay and the surrounding district – there had been a cholera epidemic in the area – and work was allowed to commence. This was all of a piece with the history of Mildmay. To quote from *Mildmay – the birth and rebirth of a unique hospital*: 'Each main advance in the history of the hospital has been preceded by calamity. It came to birth in a scourge that swept through East London; the converted warehouse in Turville Street ministered to a "turbulent mob" fleeing to Bethnal Green from the White-

---

* © Helen Taylor-Thompson 1995

chapel murders; the subsequent move to Austin Street was brought about by the demolition of the old warehouse in the LCC slum clearance, the revival of the hospital after the Second War was strengthened by its incorporation into the National Health Service, which some at the time thought might prove a disaster, and the 1965 extension, with its shift of the hospital frontage to the Hackney Road, was made possible through bomb damage resulting in a vacant site.'

Back in 1866, not far from the famous 'Oranges and Lemons' church in Austin Street, Shoreditch, lay the infamous area of the Jago, where cholera raged, killing 4,000 people in three months. The Reverend William Pennefather, a Church of England vicar in Stoke Newington, asked himself, 'What are the Christians doing to help these people?' The answer was 'nothing', until he trained some of his deaconesses in elementary nursing and sent them out into this 'no-go' district. Conditions made nursing within the homes impossible so a warehouse was taken over and a makeshift hospital materialised. As a memorial to William Pennefather, Mildmay was built on its present site and opened in 1892, nineteen years after he died.

Mildmay continued to grow and in 1948, after joining the National Health Service, its future seemed secure. The 1970s bought fresh problems to all small district general hospitals and Mildmay was no exception. From my position on the District Health Authority, I could clearly see that although Mildmay had offered to change to non-acute work, the officers saw the hospital as a potential for raising capital; if it were closed down the money both from savings in expenditure and from the sale could be used elsewhere. When the decision was finally announced, on 12th March 1984, it must to the faint-hearted have spelt the end. The Minister approved the DHA's plans to make the closure of Mildmay permanent. There was a long accompanying statement which stressed that all the possibilities had been carefully considered and that the best possible health care must be provided for the people of Tower Hamlets (but with no clear indication as to how this should be achieved); but there appeared to be no chink of light for reopening the issue.

From then on, I and three others went into action. Many ideas were discussed, a chartered accountant was employed to write a feasibility study on Mildmay becoming a community hospital, and the Minister was asked to hand back the hospital to its original owners. Before even a month had passed the Minister's response came in a letter to Peter Shore, who was the local MP and a supporter of the campaign. This time, it was positive. The Minister had no doubt been impressed by what he had heard of Mildmay's reaction to his decision. He gave his approval in principle to the reopening of the hospital, with the premises being made available to the appropriate voluntary body on a long lease at a peppercorn rent. This was all subject to the regional authority being satisfied that its proposed uses were financially viable and beneficial to the health service in Tower Hamlets.

So, after nearly forty years, Mildmay was to revert to its status as a voluntary charitable hospital. The link with the NHS, other than through ownership of the buildings, was to be severed. The financial framework within which the hospital had operated as a unit of the NHS would be totally changed, although the NHS would need to be satisfied as to the financial viability of the services the hospital would offer; but it would now be open to Mildmay to seek to recover the vision of its founders and apply it to the 1980s, with a freedom that would have been impossible had it remained within the NHS. It was apparent to all those working to reopen the hospital that most of the District Health Authority and their officers were not in favour and became exasperated. A note written at the time contained the words, 'the lady doth protest too much methinks she goes on, and ON, and ON'. Yes, this was absolutely correct, but to get things done it was the only way.

When, in 1984, the DHA and the Regional Health Authority agreed to all the proposals, we went ahead to upgrade the derelict building. It meant putting on rubber gloves, getting on our knees and scraping off the dirt. Regulations were stringent, probably more so as it was hoped we wouldn't survive long and the hospital would once again be back in the hands of the DHA for disposal. This very attitude had, of course, the effect on all involved of stimulating us to work even harder to ensure that this didn't happen.

What a wonderful day it was when, on 14th October 1985, the first patients were admitted. Only one ward had then been upgraded, but staff came from many parts of the world to nurse the patients who were to come through the doors of the new Mildmay.

Money was naturally always a problem and a great deal of thought and work went into making the needs known. Churches of all denominations now saw Mildmay as an institution well worth supporting and faithful supporters gave of their time and money and met regularly for prayer. Without the generosity of these wonderful people, and trusts and other bodies, Mildmay would never have survived.

In December 1986 history was repeated. Three men came to see me and asked, 'What are the Christians doing for people with AIDS?' As with William Pennefather, the answer was 'nothing' at that time. They asked if we would think about helping just a few terminally ill cases. After discussions with the Medical Director, a professor from the Royal London Hospital and other knowledgeable people, it became clear that there was a need, and a need that would grow. The Board took a month to deliberate over the new field of Mildmay's work and decided unanimously to go ahead and refurbish the top ward (then empty) into nine single ensuite rooms for people with AIDS. Within a few weeks the architect had produced preliminary plans and a trust provided the money for us to go to San Francisco to learn not only about what was required for an AIDS hospice, but to meet the clients and learn from them what was most beneficial. Thirteen months after the decision had been made to undertake this work, we opened Elizabeth Unit, the first hospice in Europe for people with AIDS.

Again, we had problems. Despite reassurances from the Medical Director, many people, including friends, relatives, patients and the local community, were fearful of contracting the disease and found it difficult to accept that there was no need for alarm. Bricks were thrown through the windows, local shops and pubs were reluctant to serve people from Mildmay and many of the staff and patients felt ostracised. Some supporters felt unable to continue helping, some could not accept that money was being spent on those 'who had brought it upon themselves'. Much teaching, talking and discussing went on, and indeed still does, though it appears now that people have more compassion for those suffering from AIDS.

As the number of AIDS patients grew, it was felt that a further unit should be opened. Again more money had to be found, but donations from supporters and a grant from the Department of Health enabled us to provide a further eight rooms and to open a Day Centre for those who were not so ill.

AIDS is expensive. Patients suffer from numerous illnesses, drugs are costly and nursing intensive. We specialise in particular in symptom control, to give the patient the highest quality of life possible for the time left to them. The patients and their friends are now our greatest supporters and have helped us with fundraising and putting Mildmay in the front line in the AIDS field.

It soon became apparent that the Y.C.S. (Young Chronic Sick) ward still in existence was being subsidised by £20,000 per month and this was seriously affecting the whole future of the hospital. The Board, after much thought and prayer, made the very difficult decision to close the ward; this, unfortunately, made twenty people redundant. Months later, when the financial position had been stabilised, it was agreed to specialise only in respite, rehabilitation and terminal care for people with AIDS. As a result, it was decided that the third unit would be refurbished into a further eleven single rooms, making a total of twenty-eight.

Throughout this time our Education Department was steadily increasing its work, teaching palliative care for patients with AIDS. We started to run the ENB 934 course (care and management of people with HIV and AIDS) which, I believe, was until then taught only in the teaching hospitals. People came from all over the world, some staying in the hospital in our newly upgraded rooms, which had originally been used for nurses and were in excess of our requirements. Requests came for speakers to lecture in many parts of the world; these continue to be received, but our team of experts has concentrated on Africa. These teaching sessions are usually paid for from government sources.

It was soon after opening the AIDS unit that we started to receive mothers with AIDS. It was realised that this particular group would grow, but there were no facilities for families to be together when one or more was ill. As a result, I, with Ruth Sims (Chief Executive) and Veronica Moss (Medical Director), went to New York – again through the generosity of a benefactor – to see for ourselves the plight of mothers who were dying, while their children were all affected by AIDS and many infected. In some cases the mother was dying in one hospital and their child in another, and we came back with the strong conviction that a unit for families was essential. It had been envisaged that part of the nurses' home that was no longer needed could be converted into suitable accommodation, but it soon became evident that regulations were such that only a small number of rooms could be accommodated in the original building. This would not only be insufficient for the needs but also financially unviable; it meant that we would have to demolish part of the building and rebuild.

Revenue funding was agreed with the Department of Health and it was imperative for us to open the new unit by September 1993. Revenue had already been granted and it was possible it would be withdrawn if the work was not completed by then. This gave us just nine months, but a few days before work was due to start the DHA informed us that we must not demolish the building and that if we did an injunction would be served. We had been led to believe that all appropriate approvals had been granted. Now a further delay took place until everyone was happy!

Once begun, work went on night and day. There were many frustrations and problems, but with the determination of all concerned the first six units of the Family Care Centre were opened on time. Soon the next unit will be ready, making Mildmay, with fifty-two beds, the largest hospice in Europe for people with AIDS. Her Royal Highness, the Princess of Wales, on her third visit to Mildmay, albeit in a private capacity, officially opened the £3.3 million building – Spencer Lodge, as it is now called – in Austin Street on 1st February 1994.

As Ruth Sims walked with me down Austin Street in September 1993, after the first patients had been admitted, she said that she thought we should consolidate and take a rest before embarking on any more developments. Everybody was exhausted and needed time to recuperate. Within a week there came a fax from the Director of the AIDS Commission in Uganda, asking if we would be willing to set up a centre for people with AIDS. Needless to say, we didn't hesitate. A further fax informed us that land was available in Kampala, so, in early November, Ruth Sims, Veronica Moss and I flew out there to discuss, investigate and negotiate with the Commission. We visited President Museveni and he agreed to become the Patron of Mildmay, Uganda. This all sounds very simple but there were nevertheless many problems which had to be overcome. Finance had, and indeed still has, to be found for phase one – an Outpatients Clinic for those in advanced stages of the illness. Later, a teaching centre will also be built. This may well be the start of Mildmay International, whose aim is to teach people in the Third World how to look after those dying as a result of AIDS.

Mildmay has come a long way since it reopened in 1985. We take most of our patients from the London area – 12 per cent of all who die from AIDS in the UK are cared for at Mildmay – but our influence is felt far and wide. The new Mildmay rose like a phoenix from the ashes and has grown beyond belief in the past ten years. We are confident that, with God's help, developments still on the horizon will come to fruition in the next ten years.

Chapter Eight

ACTION EVANGELISM*

•

STEVE CHALKE and NICK PAGE

Oasis is a Christian organisation working in the areas of social care, evangelism, training and media. It was formed in 1985, initially to support Steve Chalke's work as an itinerant evangelist and preacher, but since that time has grown into an organisation of some eighty full-time staff based not only in London but also in Birmingham, Sunderland, Bombay, Bangalore and Paris.

Oasis takes its mission from the words of Jesus in Luke 4:18. There, in the synagogue in his home town, Jesus quotes the words of Isaiah: 'The Spirit of the Lord is on me, because he has anointed me to preach good news to the poor. He has sent me to proclaim freedom for the prisoners and recovery of sight for the blind, to release the oppressed, to proclaim the year of the Lord's favour.' In other words, our mission as Christians is not just to talk about what we do, but to demonstrate the Christian faith by actually doing it. What Oasis aims to demonstrate is 'faith at work'. A lot of people see the Christian faith as merely a set of beliefs, a collection of ideas which don't actually have to be turned into action. In fact, nothing could be further from the truth. Belief *has* to result in action if it is to be more than empty words. So Oasis is all about demonstrating an 'holistic' gospel – a gospel which is for body, soul and spirit.

* © Steve Chalke and Nick Page 1995

Action Evangelism

From the start, Oasis has been committed to the city. Its main centre is in the heart of London, close to Waterloo station, and most of its work, whether in Bombay, Sunderland or London, takes place in the context of an urban ministry. Part of our commitment is because so many other organisations have moved out. The result is a gradual diminishing of a Christian presence in the heart of the cities of the UK. Most of the Christian activity – certainly in terms of church going – is concentrated in the so-called 'Bible belt' in the suburbs. We have always tried hard to resource and support work in the inner city.

Since its foundation, Oasis has been known as an organisation with a special ability to attract and work with teenagers and young people. This includes training them and using their time and energy in creative ways.

FRONTLINE

One of the first Oasis projects designed to equip churches in the inner city was the development of Frontline Teams. These are teams of young people based for a year in a local church, often an inner-city church suffering from a lack of people. There, they become the church's 'arms and legs', doing everything necessary to help the church grow and develop links with its local community. This might be anything from preaching or leading services, to getting involved with the youth work, or visiting.

The first Frontline Team was based in Paddington in 1987. At that time, Westbourne Park Baptist Church had only sixteen members, struggling to keep a church alive in a neighbourhood rife with drugs and a high level of unemployment. Working alongside a new minister, the six young people who formed the first ever Frontline Team embarked on a programme of reaching out to their community; this included youth work, work in schools, door-to-door visiting and starting a programme for the unemployed. In that year, sixty people made a commitment to Christ and the church started to grow again.

Since then Frontline has grown considerably. Over a hundred teams have served in various parts of the world and there is a constant demand from churches for teams to help them. Now, Frontline attracts around eighty young people each year who are based in churches not only in London but also in the West Midlands and the North East.

During their year on Frontline, all the young people spend one day a week training, through a detailed and thorough lecture and seminar programme. This allows them to learn new skills one day and put them into practice the next. The young people come from all kinds of backgrounds and have different levels of experience. Some might come from school, some from jobs, others after taking degrees or even doctorates. The one thing they have in common is a desire to get involved with the nitty-gritty of church life. Frontline provides an opportunity not only for them to give a year to God through serving the local church, but also for God to speak to them about their future. Many Frontliners have discovered gifts and skills whilst on their Frontline year which they have then gone on to develop in the future. The important thing is that through joining Frontline they have not only helped the local church but they have been given the opportunity to learn new skills and immediately put them into practice.

Indeed, this concept of practical training is at the heart of all Oasis' training programmes. It is something we take from the methods that Jesus used – training people not only by teaching them verbally, but by sending them out to get on with it. Jesus did not just sit down with people and teach them, he gave them the opportunity to go out into the world and do something. He sent them out to preach and to heal, because he knew that only by doing something ourselves do we really learn and understand. At Oasis we have always believed that it is vital to give people the opportunity to exercise gifts and take responsibility. Only then do they really start to learn and grow.

Frontline has also developed an overseas option: Frontline Teams Abroad. FTA teams go to Bombay and Bangalore in India, Moshi and Dodoma in Tanzania, Paris in France and São Paulo in Brazil. There they work alongside local churches for six months. They receive training similar to that of Frontline UK, but with the accent on cross-cultural mission.

CHRISTMAS CRACKER

Another example of our work with young people is the Christmas Cracker project. Cracker began in 1988, after a visit to India. I was appalled by the poverty and squalor there and felt impelled to do something about it. As a result we developed a project called Christmas Cracker. Young people and youth groups throughout the UK would set up a restaurant in an empty high street shop during the few weeks leading up to Christmas. In the restaurant they would serve simple food at high prices, with all the money going to relief and development work in the Third World. Under the slogan 'Eat Less – Pay More' hundreds of Cracker restaurants were set up in the years following, including many in London.

In 1991 they were succeeded by Cracker radio stations, whereby youth groups set up their own restricted-licence radio stations, this time with the slogan 'Tune In – Pay Out'. Stations were operated throughout the UK, including highly successful London projects at Deptford, Bermondsey, Wimbledon and Croydon.

Now the Cracker project has developed still further with the advent of Cracker's Really Useful Present Stores – high street shops selling fairly traded goods as Christmas presents. At Oasis we feel that the issue of fair trade is going to be an important one in the next few years. Young people in particular are now looking at how they can trade fairly with other nations, it is an issue that they feel strongly about.

TRAINING

Another aspect of our work which empowers and develops young people is our expanding role in various types of training. Along with Frontline, Oasis also runs Feet First, a two-week training course giving young people the chance to get involved in evangelism. Feet First is built around the familiar Oasis mix of learning about something and actually getting out there and doing it. It began as a project which resulted in teams of young people using creative evangelism methods on the streets of London. Now the project has expanded, with teams at ten major cities throughout the UK.

At the other end of the scale, Oasis runs two specialist courses: the Oasis Youth Ministry Course and the Oasis/Spurgeon's Church Planting and Evangelism Course. The latter, run in conjunction with Spurgeon's College, offers training for those who see themselves as evangelists or church planters, whilst the Youth Ministry Course aims to train people in all aspects of church-based youth ministry, using a mixture of training in theology, youth ministry skills and youth and community work.

One of London's biggest needs is for pastors and church planters who are committed to the city. The Oasis/Spurgeon's Church Planting and Evangelism Course aims to train church planters and evangelists to take the gospel into new areas. The churches in Britain have talked a great deal about planting new churches, but something positive needs to be done about it. Unless we train and equip people to carry out the task – and we have to recognise that church-planting requires specific skills and abilities – then progress will always be slow and sporadic. We can set all the goals and targets we want, but without people to start the hard work of planting churches we will make little progress.

My own experience of working with inner-city churches has been with two Baptist churches – Amott Road, Peckham and Haddon Hall, Bermondsey. For four years Haddon Hall was also Oasis' London base. During that time the church grew from a congregation of less than ten to one of over eighty people. Although Oasis has moved to new premises, there are still strong links with the church, notably through the development of a church resources project. The idea behind the Oasis churches project is that an experienced pastor should resource and advise the full-time staff of a number of other churches.

Pastors and church workers of inner-city churches face enormous pressures. The kinds of problems that residents of the inner city have to cope with are very different from those of the suburban churches. Problems like depression, crime, unemployment and poverty put an immense pressure on those working in the context of an inner-city church. This is why they need a high level of support and encouragement.

The Oasis Youth Ministry Course is accredited by the University of Wales and designed for committed youth ministers and youth pastors. For the two-year duration of the course, students are placed in churches where they are responsible for the development of the youth work. In this task they will naturally use ideas and techniques which they learn on the course itself. The course is taught at the Oasis London centre and most of the students are placed with London churches. At the end of the course many of the students find employment with their placement church.

SOCIAL ACTION

One of the basic tenets of Oasis' work is that communicating the gospel effectively is not just about talking to people. For a homeless person, the best example of the gospel – the 'good news' – would be a roof over their heads. Some theologians and preachers talk about evangelism and social care as two separate, but linked activities; they talk about each of them being one blade of a pair of scissors. In fact, that is a misleading analogy. Evangelism and social care simply cannot be separated, because they are both means of communicating the good news. To care for someone with the love of Christ is to tell them about Jesus – without having to use words.

From its very beginning, therefore, Oasis was set up with a concern for social care at its heart. Indeed, the name of the trust – Oasis – was originally intended as the name for a hostel for homeless people.

No. 3

The hostel did not come about until 1989 with the purchase and opening of No. 3, named after its address at 3 Cerise Road, Peckham, south London. No. 3 is a medium-stay hostel for homeless young people. The house can accommodate up to ten young people for up to a year, during which time they learn a wide variety of life skills, including budgeting, cooking and finding a job.

No. 3 is, therefore, about a lot more than just providing people with a roof over their heads. It is about giving them the training necessary to move on into secure and permanent accommodation. Many of the people who come to No. 3 have spent months on the streets; after such a time it becomes very difficult to adjust to life in a stable environment. Nor do they have the necessary skills to enable them to live independently. Housing the homeless is not just about giving someone somewhere to stay, it is also about providing them with the skills necessary to look after themselves.

No. 3 offers two levels of accommodation – either single room or bedsit – depending on the resident's experience and ability. Most will progress from communal living to more independence in a bedsit. From there it is hoped that they will go on to find permanent accommodation of their own.

Part of the appeal of No. 3 also lies in its family atmosphere; the staff try very hard to make No. 3 a home. Many of the residents have come from institutional care of one kind or another and have experienced disrupted family lives: what they need is not a hostel, but a home.

MOBILE CARE UNIT AND STREET TEAMS

No. 3 was the first Oasis social care project, but was soon followed by the development of Street Teams and the Mobile Care Unit. The Street Teams are groups of volunteers, co-ordinated from the Oasis London Centre in Blackfriars Road, near Waterloo. They go out each weekday night and their aim is simply to make contact with the homeless on the streets. Street Team members are Christians from many different churches in the city who want to try to do something about the problems of homelessness. They are not professionals, but they do receive training and support to help them in their work.

The work of the Street Teams is backed up by the Mobile Care Unit which is a converted double-decker bus. On the Mobile Care Unit the homeless can obtain free drinks, as well as advice and a listening ear. There is also a mobile phone, which enables them to ring around to find hostel places for the night. The bus has become a well-known sight on the streets of London – a visible reminder that Christianity is about action as well as words.

'LIZZIE'S'

In 1993 Oasis added to these projects with the opening of the Elizabeth Baxter Health Centre – or 'Lizzie's', as it is more affectionately known. Lizzie's is a drop-in primary health-care centre which allows homeless people access to the health care they so desperately need. For many homeless people it is difficult to get access to a GP, because to register with a GP you often need an address. Often if homeless people are in need of medical attention they have to go to a hospital accident and emergency unit, which may mean a long wait. Lizzie's offers them a place where they can get immediate attention and gain access to a GP.

The health centre has nursing staff, chiropody services

and laundry and hygiene facilities. Homeless people can have a shower and obtain a full set of clean clothes. Oasis is also aiming to develop a nutritional research project and a resettlement course in life skills.

Soon Oasis hopes to develop its work still further with the purchase of a large semi-detached house in Streatham, which has been divided into bedsits. This will provide permanent, low-cost, good-quality housing with support from a social care worker on site. The idea, again, is not just to provide somewhere to live, but also to teach the skills necessary to live an independent life.

OASIS OVERSEAS

Oasis' social care is not limited to Britain; the project has always been involved with development work overseas. Now, however, this work has increased with the opening of a centre in Bombay, India. The Oasis India Centre not only houses and co-ordinates the Frontline Teams who arrive each year, but also promotes ongoing social-care projects in the form of Jacob's Well and work with street children.

JACOB'S WELL
Jacob's Well is a project run by Oasis to provide training and employment for disadvantaged and marginalised women, particularly ex-prostitutes. Using the skills of professional fashion designers and drawing on traditional Indian designs and materials, Jacob's Well aims to produce high-quality garments and accessories for marketing in Britain. Once again, the issue of fair trade lies at the heart of what Oasis is doing. Jacob's Well will not only trade goods, but will also provide jobs and training for women in dire need of a way out of the poverty trap.

Action Evangelism

STREET CHILDREN

Oasis has also started projects to help street children in Bombay and in Bangalore. In Bombay, we are working with the 'railway children' – children whose only home is the area around the railway stations. Oasis runs an orphanage and an open-air school in both cities and in Bangalore has started a project for the 'rag pickers' – children who eke out a precarious living by scavenging through the dumps for rags or other items that they can sell.

COMMUNICATION AND MEDIA

It was Dietrich Bonhoeffer who posed the question, 'How do we speak in a secular way about God?' Along with our work in training and social care, Oasis has an expanding role in communicating the message of the Christian faith to those who need to hear it, in a language that they can understand. In evangelism, Oasis was one of the first Christian organisations to start using video technology to talk about Jesus. The Video Express shows, and then the sixteen-screen Video Wall shows, use pop and rock videos and film clips to illustrate the message. The idea is simply to talk to people – and particularly young people – in the language of their own culture.

CAPITAL RADIATE

In partnership with the London Baptist Association, Oasis also runs Capital Radiate – a project designed to co-ordinate youth work in the 270 Baptist churches in London, as well as to train and motivate young people. Among the many projects that Capital Radiate has set up was Concept Cafes – a chain of thirty non-alcoholic cocktail bars opened throughout London in the summer of 1992. The idea was to offer a creative and welcoming venue for evangelism. Again, the emphasis was on speaking people's own language, using bands and videos.

ON FIRE AND FIRED UP

Oasis was also the leading light behind the national evangelistic initiative 'On Fire', which saw thousands of churches – hundreds of them based in London – use the festival of Pentecost 1994 as a chance to invite their community to join them in celebrating the birthday of the church. Churches held carnivals, parties, processions and fireworks parties, all designed to communicate with their community in a relevant and non-threatening way.

Accompanying 'On Fire' was 'Fired Up', the youth arm of the project. Young people who took part in 'Fired Up' not only became involved in evangelism, but also collected over 77,500 thumb prints for a massive petition urging the Government to take action over the plight of the world's street children. The petition was delivered to the Prime Minister, John Major, in summer 1994. They also organised activities which raised an estimated £100,000.

TELEVISION, RADIO AND VIDEO

Another way in which Oasis is using the media is in an increasing involvement with television. Working in the centre of London gives Oasis easy access to the world of television, much of which is based in the capital. Not only does our work engender a lot of interest from TV companies – who wish, for example, to film at Lizzie's or on the bus – but also we are increasingly involved in creating television programmes ourselves. Steve's regular work as a presenter on GMTV – the national breakfast show which goes out on the ITV network – has created opportunities to speak out on issues such as marriage, relationships, debt and parenting.

In 1994 we promoted a 'Motivation Weekend', which encouraged individuals and groups throughout the country to do sponsored keep-fit and aerobic sessions. All the money raised – over £500,000 in all – was sent to India to build hospitals and clinics in the area devastated by the earthquake of 1993.

Along with the television work, Oasis staff are frequently to be found on local and national radio. We also run a full-time press office, providing news and information both to the Christian press and to the national and local secular media. All this gives us a unique opportunity to speak out on issues that really matter, offering a Christian perspective and practical advice on down-to-earth problems.

1995 – OASIS' TENTH BIRTHDAY

1995 will see the tenth anniversary of Oasis. In that time it has grown from the idea of one man to a team of hundreds of people in centres spanning the globe. But our commitment to the city remains constant. Whether on the streets of Bombay or Bermondsey, Oasis is committed to showing faith at work, and that means taking the gospel to those who really need to hear it.

When God said he loved us, he meant it. He made a sacrifice and became part of our world. Today, two thousand years on, the world deserves more from the Church than empty words and theological debate. What we have to do is get our hands dirty, get involved and take action. What we have to do is show faith at work.

Chapter Nine

COMMUNITY REGENERATION*

●

ANDREW MAWSON

HOW DID IT START?

'Church-goers watched in horror as a vicar taking a service collapsed at the altar and later died... in front of a packed congregation.' So read the headline of the *East London Advertiser* on 6th May 1983. The reality was somewhat different. The Reverend Bill Barker, a retired minister, had in fact collapsed in the pulpit whilst addressing a congregation of ten elderly people. The Reverend David Moore, the local Methodist Superintendent minister, was called in to deal with the crisis and it was through his intervention and willingness to recognise an opportunity, where many saw only a problem, that a relationship was established between this small United Reformed church and the local Methodist Circuit. Both realised that this death was a portent of what the congregation might very soon face itself if imaginative steps were not taken to grasp the future.

I begin writing this chapter some ten years on, having just received a letter from Dr Brian Mawhinney, the Secretary of State for Health, informing me that the first £500,000 has now been agreed towards a new £1.2 million health centre, in the form of a cloister, at the rear of our present buildings. This primary health-care facility, and the 3–acre park and

* © Andrew Mawson 1995

the land surrounding it, will, for the first time in Britain, bring together the arts, education, the environment and health in an integrated community development in the heart of the East End of London. This chapter attempts to record and highlight those events during the last decade which have brought about these possibilities in one of the most deprived areas of London, during one of the most turbulent political decades in living memory. This urban project recognised the end of an era, marked by the Thatcher years, and was concerned not simply to carp but to explore a new model of community development at a time in the early 1980s when 'society' and 'community' were dirty words.

This is inevitably a personal account and no doubt some who have shared the journey would record it differently. I hope that this narrative will bring to the surface the people and events who have formed the seed bed in the East End of London for what has now become known as the Bromley by Bow Centre.

The Bromley by Bow United Reformed Church, as it was then known in 1984, had a congregation of ten elderly members, large run-down Free Church buildings and an uncertain future. Historically the church had known happier times at the centre of a group of East End estates. Before the Second World War it had run a large Boys' Brigade, built upon the traditional, if not limited, contacts with the few church-goers in the surrounding area. Extensive war damage meant the demolition of the old church building and the rebuilding, in 1958, of a new church. This traditional design expected life to continue much as it had done before the war. It did not, and the trend of the population to move east out of Tower Hamlets accelerated.

The small elderly congregation that survived into the 1980s gradually lost all real contact with the surrounding area. The new multi-cultural community which replaced the more traditional East End families had little connection with the church and few reasons to join. Arriving, as an outsider, one cold November night in 1983 at a meeting with the remaining ten elderly church members who were huddled around a useless radiator in a derelict church hall, was like entering a time warp, somewhere in the 1950s.

This was the time of the Anglican Report *Faith in the City*, when the churches of Britain, confronted with the 'Thatcherite' years, felt they must act in the inner city priority areas of the United Kingdom. Bill Barker's death had provided the opportunity for David Moore to establish a relationship with this small congregation. He immediately recognised the potential of what were derelict buildings in a local community with little practical communal space. Bromley by Bow, at the eastern edge of the borough, suffered greatly from under-funding and a lack of resources. There was good reason why the church should be seen to act in this forgotten corner of inner London.

Discussions followed between the Methodist Circuit and the Thames North Province of the United Reformed Church to see if an ecumenical package could be produced, which would enable a three-year experiment to begin. I was approached by John Kennedy, a friend whom I had known through my involvement in Central America in the early 1980s, to see if I would be willing to be considered for the post. This presented a problem because, only days before, I had accepted a call to a church in Birmingham. Clearly the possibilities for this church excited me, and within the year my wife and I made the hard decision to pull up our shallow roots in Birmingham and accept the call to the East End – an untidy process but one that we knew was right.

It is true to say that there were no grand plans when I arrived in Bow, simply instinct that this might be the place to be at this moment. In this forgotten corner one experienced sharply the alienation of the church from the mainstream of our society. Here the church was not protected by the veneer of just enough financial resources and personnel to delude itself into believing that we could carry on much as we had in the past. This was not an option and we all knew it. A radical rethink of what this church was about was called for.

Gordon McLaren, our architect and close friend and advisor, told me once that the reason he chose to live among the tower blocks of Tower Hamlets and the 'jumble sale' of British architecture by this time appearing on the Isle of Dogs was because here one could see most clearly where British architecture was at. Not for him the renovated, gentrified Victorian dwellings in Islington. In many senses Bromley by Bow illustrated starkly not only the state of architecture but also the true position of the Church in modern Britain and few seemed capable of grasping the disturbing reality.

Once the Induction Service was over, and all my supporters had disappeared, I was left alone in large cold church buildings, reflecting upon my fate and wondering what on earth I should do. There were no clear signs. So unsure was I about what I would fill the day doing that within weeks I experienced resistance to rising early.

One elder, who was the church caretaker, showed me around the derelict rooms one wet afternoon. She showed me the Boys' Brigade 'Rifle Room', as it was affectionately known, full of memorabilia from days long since gone. On entering the dark space I was immediately conscious of a damp atmosphere. The windows were bricked up and I was told not to touch the light switch, which was obviously wet. Looking into this windowless abyss, I was informed that there was a piano at the far end. I paddled across the floor, finding my way between discarded objects, and eventually discovered the outline of the instrument. It was polished every Thursday, so I learnt. I lifted the lid only to find the keys solid, due to expansion. No music had been played here for many years; the instrument was a parable of the church.

I decided that what was needed was a monastic approach to life – an order, a rhythm to the day, if only for the sake of survival. In the mornings, I decided, I would try to meet other people, through whatever contacts I could establish locally. The afternoon would then be spent teaching myself the piano on the one instrument that did work, on the derelict stage in the church hall. (This was made somewhat difficult by the absence of middle 'C', but I persevered!) I also set about preparing a new hymn book and liturgy to move us beyond the dull hymn sandwich which so many churches still seem prepared to perform each Sunday. My experience of liturgy at the Northern Baptist College and later at the John Bunyan Baptist Church, in Kingston-upon-Thames, had opened up the treasures of the liturgical tradition and I wanted to explore further.

I soon noticed that every time I appeared in the church hall in an afternoon so did the caretaker. She would sweep the floor as I walked over it. I was confused, my shoes seemed to be clean. Mary would look inquiringly at me playing the piano alone on the stage. Surely I should be doing something more constructive? Mary (not her real name), I was soon to discover, was a timid woman whose life revolved around the care of these derelict premises. I began to notice odd items disappearing, objects of no value. When I eventually raised the subject with another elder I was told, with a knowing look, that it was Mary and that if I was patient the items would reappear, if I mentioned their loss. Sure enough they did.

This was my first real insight into the human realities of this small, closed and anachronistic community. Love and charity meant that Mary was not to be upset. Her illness had to be lived with, particularly since it seemed that some years earlier she had been arrested at a local shop for theft. I learned over the years to appreciate Mary's timid ways for she had an innate instinct for worship and the liturgy. She took great care in preparing the church for Sunday service and – now she has moved east to live near her only surviving daughter – I miss her presence at evening prayers.

I tell this tale simply to illustrate the complex human reality I had entered, in which the church simply echoed the needs of the wider human community outside our doors. The church had become the home for a few elderly people who, for one reason or another, had been unable to join the thousands of people who moved east in the years following the Second World War.

The afternoon Sunday service at this time consisted of me standing behind the communion table on the raised dais, offering my words of wisdom to ten elderly people at least twice my age. The congregation sat separately on the twenty long pews that made up the church, in the places which had seemingly been reserved for them. It looked from the front as though the dead had been carried out and those remaining had failed to notice the spaces where once they sat. At the back of the church was a window in the wall through which coffins had to be passed. Apparently the side doors involved too acute an angle for coffins to negotiate comfortably. The exterior windows had panes of frosted glass, the front door was made of solid oak and the walls were grey and dusty. To all intents and purposes, to passers-by we were closed for business.

My first real contact with the local community came through Ann and her partner, Dave. They asked me to baptise their daughter, Sarah, and I agreed on the condition that we write the liturgy together and that every year, during the first few years of Sarah's life, on the anniversary of her baptism, I be allowed to come to their flat and share with them in a small liturgy to mark her birth. They agreed. This annual event involved the lighting of a candle, shared written prayers, cakes and coffee. Dave initially was quite suspicious of the church, for good reason. But as we got to know one another and he realised that I wasn't simply out to evangelise, our relationship became established. In the early years these baptismal anniversaries became numerous and gave me important and significant contacts with families within the local community, many of which continue today. Sarah is now eleven and passes the church with her mother each Sunday morning on her way to Tesco, as I prepare the liturgy. We see each other through the glass front door and sometimes she waves.

This initial experience persuaded me to adopt a policy of writing the liturgy for all baptisms, weddings and funerals (where possible) with the families and those involved. It meant a lot of work but I was determined that the church would not simply be an extension of Tesco, across the road, providing the rites of passage on demand. There was enough confusion locally with the Anglican policy, and I was concerned to give people time and explain what we were about. This proved healthy for all concerned, and out of this process some deep and important relationships have grown over the years. Some of the best liturgies were not written by me. I was simply the president, ensuring that all was done in good order and that people were made aware of the rich treasures of the church's liturgical tradition.

I told people that if God existed (and I admitted that the question was a real one) then she or he might be more concerned about the truth of what we did and said in church, rather than simply parroting the correct words. This was always understood and welcomed as a way of thinking about the task in hand. I encouraged people to use any gifts of music, poetry and so on that they possessed, incorporating their musical tastes within the liturgical form. In a secular culture this usually meant recorded modern music, but I have often been surprised by people's creativity when given the space to experiment. I recall one rendering of 'When the red, red robin goes bob-bob-bobbing along', played on the recorder by a couple and their friends, at the baptism of their son Robin.

Over the years I have presided over a number of unusual liturgies. One began in the church and ended on Glastonbury Tor, with a shared chalice of wine and a very mixed group of New Age Travellers. I have often been astounded at the amounts of money East Enders spend in preparing for these rites of passage and the beautiful costumes which adorn their children. There is an instinctive sense of what counts, even if, on occasions, it sometimes feels a little over the top. Few liturgies have not worked and I think the congregation would not think it an exaggeration when I say that occasionally we have glimpsed through them something of the transcendent. Occasionally too the past, present and future aspirations of a community, their hopes and their fears have been brought together, articulated and celebrated in such a way that text and context danced together. Over the years I have become more persuaded than ever of the profound and unique gift of liturgy which we, the churches, possess, to share with the communities within which we are set, and I am often saddened by the sometimes arid attempts of liturgical commissions to engage authentically with this process. Authentic liturgy, in my view, can only arise when the church is fully engaged in the political, social and cultural life of a community and society.

None of the above is particularly radical or new. It was for me simply a concrete mechanism by which I could start to share in the life of this East End community, which itself shared in none of the churches' worlds. Exegesis was my ongoing task, to open up and explore the connections between a historic faith and the community in which we live. The chalice and plate, purchased from the Taize Community in France and placed on the altar at the centre of our present buildings for all to see, embody this tension.

I realise, ten years on, that we have not in any way changed the alienation, on a wider scale, that the working class feel towards the Church. These historic processes have constantly borne down upon us and we have made little visible impact. My concern has been to identify 'moments' rather than epoch-making changes. In the hustle and bustle of life I have consciously encouraged people to embrace their own spirituality through the 'moments in time and space' that we shared together, to stop and reflect upon the profound possibilities of all human life. East Enders are practical people, so theological ideas have always been focused, where possible, on concrete acts – perhaps the lighting of a candle, the sign of the light of a new-born child, full of potential and newness, coming into the world, or a photograph for a board entitled 'Moments in Time' which would remind children and parents in later days of those moments in history as their own time moved on and the God who is active in history moved on with them. I am conscious that there is much more to say after ten years of experimentation, but these few reflections, I hope, give a taste of how days began to be filled and contacts made as a minister or priest, like many others, struggled for relevance in an often alien secular world.

In 1984 our extensive buildings were used for only two hours each week. For the 3 pm service on a Sunday and for the fortnightly Labour Party meeting. They too were a small group with little real support. I often mused on the historical connections between us and how we both were involved in the belief business and yet both had little actual success. Our day had apparently come and gone, time had moved on and both our structures had failed to move with it. It was clear to me that history had landed this church with this set of buildings and that we had better share them, if nothing else, with a neighbourhood which had so few community facilities. The first real opportunity came when Mary Mallinson approached me in early 1985, in her search for premises for the emerging 'Out and About' group. Tower Hamlets has a high proportion of disabled people, many of whom have few support structures and no transport. 'Out and About' was to become the main voluntary-sector facility for people with disabilities in the borough. At this time Mary had been given a grant of £10,000 to spend, which was seen as serious money, and we agreed with the members to renovate a small room for an office and to build a set of new conveniences, including a toilet for the disabled. We also agreed a policy of working together rather than simply operating a tenant and landlord arrangement.

Mary introduced me to Ann Wyatt, her architect, who was eventually to become responsible for the redesign of all the buildings, with her husband, Gordon. Ann died a few years later after giving birth to their second child, who also died within hours. Ann's death and the funeral service, which was conducted amid scaffolding and building development, was the historic moment when a soul entered our community. As many diverse people shared in the grief of this young family, I reflected upon the tragedy that was taking place. A beautiful triptych now stands in the quiet room overlooking the church and Ann's story has joined numerous others as part of the narrative of the community.

At the church meeting, when this initial phase of development was first mooted, I suggested to the members that we should adopt a spirit of openness to all potential users of the premises – that we should say 'yes' to everyone, unless we had a very good reason to say 'no'. This was unanimously agreed. We also adopted a policy that any groups using space would have to agree to work together, the view being that our shared strength was always greater than our individual interests. Many groups welcomed this opportunity and benefited financially from it. The members were realistic and recognised that we had nothing to lose, we were in a live-or-die situation and so we had better live dangerously. This spirit of adventure and openness was to prove a great asset and defined a community culture that still exists to this day.

It became clear to me that we must use what 'assets' we had to engage with a community where all real contact had been lost. There was no master plan, simply an instinct that this might prove to be a way forward. I began to realise that the church buildings would need to be viewed with a businessman's eye and that an entrepreneurial spirit, no matter how that term had been commandeered by right-wing politicians, would be required. If we did not search for opportunities for life we would certainly embrace a speedy, undignified death.

The local estates, I soon discovered, were constantly leafleted by one group or another, demanding people's allegiance, be it the Labour Party, the emerging Liberal Democrat Party, the evangelical Christians or the Jehovah's Witnesses. All sought to engage with people's beliefs but none was willing to wait. Instant responses were required and they were received, in that 95 per cent of all leaflets went straight in the bin. Clearly this local community would require a more sustained and personal approach, with no hidden agendas. People should not be treated as fodder for other people's clubs and institutions.

I was also becoming increasingly conscious, on a wider front, that many of the old political/social and religious institutions in our society were becoming more and more irrelevant to many people's lives. The church was clearly not the only dinosaur whose days were numbered. But where would the new sense of a corporate identity come from in a country that was being told that there was no such thing as society? The Labour Party, the historic bastion of such beliefs, seemed to have lost its way; there was no corporate vision, no sense of what it meant to be a community. The socialist experiment was collapsing before our eyes, yet still some talked as though nothing had changed in Britain. I knew it had and that we must explore afresh what community might mean for this new era. I observed that private living, behind the iron security doors, increasingly led to isolation, fear and mental ill health. It was also true that East End youngsters were spending hundreds of pounds at the Roman Road market buying identical clothes, the uniform of their generation, supposedly to proclaim their individuality. I wrote an article at the time for a German magazine and entitled it 'The rich get richer and the poor buy videos'. There are in fact more video machines per head of population in Tower Hamlets than anywhere else in the country. What was this saying about the processes of privatisation proclaimed from Downing Street and what did it mean for a faith built upon the corporate imagery of the body of Christ? It was the connections that fascinated me, the answer must come from others.

It became clear within the first three years that we must build upon the foundations of personal relationships and practical initiatives, rather than join the paper train. I also began to recognise that people were very parochial and that many feared change. A central question was how to unlock these years of inertia.

During my first few months I was encouraged by John Kennedy, a Methodist colleague, to experiment with a series of public discussions on marriage and the family. I prepared an amusing leaflet entitled 'Marriage is magic: it turns princes into frogs' and distributed it to two thousand homes. No one turned up – a salutary lesson in a video culture where communication was through images and not words, monologue and not dialogue. If I was to relate to these people we would have to do better than this!

I was introduced to Santiago Bell by a friendly journalist whom I knew through my work on Central America and Liberation Theology during the early 1980s. Santiago is a Chilean exile who once worked with the famous educationalist Paulo Freire and had paid the price of putting this theology to work. He had been responsible for establishing various community initiatives in Chile during the Allende administration. A former governor of a province, Santiago was arrested in 1973, following the coup d'etat, tortured and imprisoned along with thousands of others.

In prison he was ordained a deacon and called to share a humble liturgy of bread and water with his nine companions. Through this meal he kept his sanity whilst being brutally humiliated. In an article in *The Independent on Sunday*, written for our exhibition at the Concourse Gallery in the Barbican in 1993, Santiago recalled how he had been beaten and tortured and forced into near madness in solitary confinement: 'They made me eat shit with a spoon. People say that this has made me wise. Well, I would rather be stupid and not have had the lesson. I learnt things but they were all dark things.' Strangely that darkness has shed much light in Bow.

Because his paternal grandfather was Scottish, Santiago and his wife and six children were eventually released into exile in Britain. His life destroyed, he was now reduced to doing odd jobs in people's houses. When we first met I instantly recognised his artistic potential. His portfolio presented a master craftsman who was capable of earning a large salary in the West End. He asked simply for a workshop space to continue his craft and one that could be open to members of the local community. It was clear that this creative process he was initiating would also be the route through which he would find his own healing. The church members unanimously agreed to give Santiago a derelict space to the side of the church hall. Within weeks he had turned it into an orderly workshop with beautifully designed hand-made benches, which echoed the attention to detail of his art. It was not long before the congregation also recognised his priestly gifts and this renegade Catholic was invited by the members to share in my ministry and administer here, as he had done in prison, the sacred mysteries.

We had no money and for the first eight months Santiago earned nothing. He simply opened his door and began work. We undertook no publicity, Santiago's view being that the community would discover this oasis for itself. He was right. One of the first people to come was a young man called Daniel who lived in a squat next door. He was building eccentric furniture for Janet Street-Porter's house and needed Santiago's skill and tools to complete the commission. Santiago obliged and the first relationship was established, amid suspicions as to what I was exactly about.

Daniel was followed by his near neighbour, Su, a young woman requiring space to build a small sailing boat. She asked for permission to use the derelict hall. Ethel, an elderly member, with her usual youthful spirit suggested to the church meeting that Noah built a boat so why shouldn't Su do so in our hall. This seemed a perfectly reasonable line of argument to me. Through the process of building the boat our relationship became established. Su, I soon discovered, had encountered a zealous Pentecostalist teacher at school who had tried to convert her; this had led her, a bright girl, to be totally suspicious of anything Christian. It was some considerable time before she could fully trust that Santiago and I had no hidden agenda. Certainly our early conversations over afternoon tea in her house, viewing the magnificent greenhouse under plastic, which Ebon, who shared the home, had constructed, were memorable times.

The real break-through came when one morning I arrived to find a small jar of flowers on the floor outside the workshop door. On a note was written 'With many thanks for the use of the workshop, wild flowers of Bow, Su.' Here was a kindred spirit. Su may have had little time for the church, but she certainly rang bells with both Santiago and me. The first important community relationship outside the church membership had taken root. Her insight and connections were to prove crucial in the months ahead, for Su was to point us to the real possibilities that lay on the doorstep.

It was during these months that I became increasingly convinced that the role of the church in such urban areas, where high-rise living produced a dehumanising privatisation of life, must be as a catalyst to bring together in concrete ways the variety of people who lived cheek by jowl and yet often seemed unaware of each other. Surely to create community was an historic calling of the Church. To establish a human context, a space, which people could enter and explore together the connections that existed between them – was not this theology in action? I was also now encountering considerable pastoral demands. I could not cope alone; we needed a corporate response to be effective.

I became concerned to create a concrete environment in which ordinary people's lives, from diverse racial backgrounds, would cross and interact. Care was taken not to control the interplay but to create the arena in which real human integration, that was visibly evolving, could take place. The cafe, the dance school, the workshops and the nursery have many tales to tell of this growing integration, amid the inevitable conflicts that occasionally resulted between both individuals and groups. On the whole the experience has been friendly and open and people have been generous with each other. The church's position was clear: we supported an equal opportunities policy and were open to all people of whatever race or creed. When local parents refused to join in the local Muslim Eid festival at the school and withdrew their children, we purposely attended. The church has since hosted numerous Bengali festivals and Muslim prayers in the church space where the Eucharist is shared. We conclude each Sunday liturgy with the words: 'Living God, we thank you for this heavenly banquet prepared for us and all the peoples of the earth.' The message, in a context where there is serious racial tension, is clear among locals who know us. Others of a more traditional Christian mindset worry considerably about this policy. We have also sought to take an independent political stand. Our view has been, in a changing climate, that a bird with one wing never flies. We have remained vigilant and open.

If the role of the church was not simply to gain members but to recognise that 'grace is everywhere' then our actions had to communicate this mystery. To be ecumenical (which literally means 'of the whole inhabited earth' in the true sense of this word) we had to engage with the real world, not expend our energy on claiming the world for Christ but rather help the world to see what was already his! Could we trust each other enough for dialogue to take place in what many of us knew was a totally new historical context where the old rules had become increasingly irrelevant? Language – and what we meant by what we said – was ironically the serious barrier to communication. The Church, like many other groups, plays its own language game which is often meaningless outside its walls. We must speak through actions. Following the famous dictum of St Francis, we must go into the whole world and preach the gospel and, if we have to, say something.

It would be dishonest not to admit that the middle classes locally have had an important part to play in all the developments of Bow. Without them we would never have started. One of my concerns about much of the Liberation Theology I had witnessed in action in Central America was the often unstated role that this social group played in any social change. They were the ones who were economically flexible enough to engage in social change. 'The poor', I observed, usually had too many pressing demands placed upon them to be able to change their lot in any real way. Indeed, experience often led them to be fatalistic.

I realised that we needed to bring together a creative mix from the new diversity of life that was now evolving in east London. The compartmentalisation of local communities was a reality, be they working class, middle class, the elderly, the young, the New Age Travellers or the Bengali youths. People on the whole had few opportunities where their lives could truly cross and engage, creating understanding and tolerance. The irony of the neighbourhood system of local government, introduced during this time by the Liberal Democrats, is that it often exacerbates the mindset of the ghetto.

I recall that Ethel, an elderly member of the church, was initially very suspicious of Su, who lived in what she saw as a derelict squat and who seemed to have little in common with her East End grandchildren. When their lives became connected through Su's involvement in the workshop they became good friends. Both once remarked to me, within days of each other and quite independently, what a special person they thought the other was. I was amused!

This example may seem insignificant to the outsider, but my awareness of the isolation of some people's lives and the misplaced hostility to other groups, led me to believe that this was an important step forward. Contradictory experience was now let loose within the community, which challenged the prevailing assumptions of many. The fact that Jane, a local schizophrenic, is greeted by other people at the shops and now shares food with others in our cafe is a major miracle. In the early days I recall young boys making fun of her unusual features and behaviour. Now the potential exists for Jane to be a person in her own right. The careful work of Allison Trimble has meant that Jane is known more widely, and her difficulties, through group work with local women, are now a little understood. Indeed, her illness has helped others cope with their own disabilities, for all of us have them.

WHERE ARE WE NOW?

It seems important to catalogue the early years in terms of simple memories in order to provide clues to the pattern of development that has taken place since. Now we must move into the present and outline the main components of the project that have resulted from these initial murmurings. There never was a grand plan, or an empire envisaged; each part of the project developed for quite pragmatic reasons and all the church did was to offer space.

The continual changes in administration in the local authority, coupled with financial and administrative incompetence, force us to live daily with the possibility of collapse. Building a project such as this is very much like attempting to build a house on sand, with the tide never far away. What I shall now describe must be understood within this financial context.

Both Santiago and I have always known, since the early days, that the project was about the present; we said that it was not 'for ever'. What matters is not the building of an edifice which outlasts us all, but to live life to the full now. When I eventually leave Bow I would like to say that we played the game with some success; now let someone else appear and possibly build something different. This would not be a sign of failure, but a realistic response to the fast-moving and unpredictable environment in which we are living. The worship area itself is designed as a tent, the pegs can be easily pulled out. The project as a whole is simply a movement in time and space; let us enjoy it for what it is.

The Bromley by Bow Centre, as we are now known, has today become a unique venture at the crossroads of community, the arts, education, health, environment and liturgy. The formerly derelict buildings have been extended and are now used by over 600 people each week. We employ a staff of forty and run a budget in excess of £700,000. Until recently the project has been very local, but we are now faced with the pros and cons of increasing national significance. Today the Centre comprises the following elements: a range of art workshops; a Bengali language project; a nursery; a toy library; creche facilities; a community cafe; an art gallery; a church; until recently the Janet Viola School of modern dance; a health project; offices; a community garden.

We have in recent years hosted a visit by HRH the Princess of Wales, along with three government ministers and the permanent secretary from the Home Office. We are now embarking upon a 3-acre park development which will include a new health centre to provide the main primary health care for the area. Until now local GPs have operated in run-down premises and it has proved impossible to attract high-quality doctors into the area. This integrated development, we hope, will address this problem. Over the years I have buried some who have died before their time who, had they received adequate primary health care, might still have been alive today. It is hoped that this initiative will be a practical response to this human need.

The policy of the Centre today remains one of enabling. We aim to make concrete those ideas which would otherwise remain only potentials within the community. We have embraced creativity and artistic endeavour as central to the task. Tower Hamlets has probably the largest artistic community outside New York and we have sought consciously to engage this community in our model of urban regeneration. We now run art workshops in stained glass, woodwork, stone sculpture, pottery, life drawing, wood sculpture and mosaics. We have had gallery space in the City of London and in 1993 we held an exhibition in the Concourse Gallery, at the Barbican; two hundred works of art were on display, provided by local people and professional artists. Lord Ennals and Lord Peyton, to whom I will always be grateful, hosted two private views sponsored by British Gas and the Post Office. Pentecost '95 and The Great Banquet were launched at this event.

We have been concerned to design helpful spaces in which people can live and work, recognising the truth that we are all profoundly influenced by the physical spaces that we occupy. I have increasingly come to the conclusion that our built environment deeply affects the way people live and behave in the inner cities. Alice Coleman in *Utopia on Trial*[1] all too clearly demonstrates this fact. The spaces in Bow have therefore been designed as artistic expressions in themselves.

We have an unusual approach to organising our artistic work, by which we encourage local artists, who are committed to working with local people, to work from the Centre. Establishing their studio space on site creates a sense of openness and also enables the project to have a 'critical mass' of artistic activity. We also now work extensively with people with disabilities, enabling them to explore their artistic talents alongside significant local artists and volunteers. The integrated nature of these workshops reflects the diversity of the local community and prevents making ghettos of people labelled by their particular problem. One group has, for example, made a set of ceramic plant pots for the garden they helped to design and build. The garden has won local prizes as well as the Shell Better Britain Award for the London Region. In September 1991 the garden was

---

[1] Alice Coleman, *Utopia on Trial: Vision and Reality in Planned Housing*, H. Shipman, 1990.

formally opened by Mrs Carey, the wife of the Archbishop of Canterbury. Dr Carey was born locally and some of the plants come from Lambeth Palace, the second largest private garden in London.

The liturgical space stands at the centre of the buildings and is surrounded by an art gallery, a day nursery, a toy library and creche facilities. This unusual and flexible area converts quickly into a theatre or large open space. Courses have been run in this context on a wide range of topics, including parenting and child-birth (sponsored by the Body Shop), and singing classes are held twice each week. Stephen Goode, a local parent, and his wife, Yvonne Begley, were responsible for developing our child-care facilities initially from a small co-operative nursery that they ran from their home. The nursery, now under the able management of Jo Monteith-Hodge, is still run by the parents. Ten years on, at a recent AGM, parents were asking if their children could remain until they were five because they recognised how important this facility had become in their children's development. One parent indicated that she did not know of any other nursery facility which mixed children's play with the arts, culture and community at such an early age. Clearly the integrated philosophy of the nursery, developed initially by Stephen and Yvonne and at the time resisted by Social Services, has now become recognised in its own right. Finbar, the last of their four children, is now to move on to infant school, but they have left us with a legacy, a model of child care, which offers lessons for the future.

The project is multi-cultural and has people involved from every corner of the globe. In 1990 we published a book on education entitled *A World of Schools*, written by Sister Helen Down's Write Back Team. Contributions from twenty-seven local people articulated their experience of education in countries very different from our own. Our research demonstrated that over fifty languages and dialects were spoken within ten minutes' walk of our buildings. Lord Ennals, in the Foreword to the book, described Bromley by

Bow as 'a mini United Nations amid the tower blocks of Tower Hamlets'.

The Centre is committed to an open-access, equal-opportunities policy. We employ staff from different religious backgrounds, since we rejected the idea of just employing Christians in favour of a broader ecumenical view. This rich mix has created a fertile soil for human interaction. For example, we employ Zenith, who is a Muslim and a very capable Bengali outreach worker. With her innate entrepreneurial skills she was given the freedom to explore our relationship with the growing Bengali population (now nearly one third of the total) moving east out of Whitechapel. We now work with over a hundred families and at the most recent Eid festival it was moving to watch Ethel, now our oldest church member, giving the prizes to the Bengali children with a kiss. We had come a long way. This year a group of East End women and their Bengali counterparts have taken part in Project Sinai together. The husbands have given permission and what were two quite distinct groupings are now becoming increasingly integrated.

As a project we have developed considerable skills in administration and fundraising. Donald Findley, the Assistant Director responsible for Finance, has brought to us the support of many charitable trusts, the local authority and industry. Donald also takes upon himself all our financial worries, giving the rest of us the freedom to get on with the job. Few realise, I suspect, how truly liberating this can be. We run a tight budget and in the past have resisted employing caretakers, receptionists, secretaries, and other necessary back-up staff, doing much of the administrative work ourselves. This is now changing as we grow in size. We work democratically, but with a minimum of paper work. Trust has been crucial in giving each of the very capable senior staff room to manoeuvre. We are now accountable to an Executive Board which brings together local people, the church and the business community in a creative mix. I suspect that it is rare in our society that top business people share with local people the responsibility for running such an enterprise. The management structure, like the project itself, seeks to break down the compartments that so many of us have to operate within. Today the project is about making connections with the diverse aspects of community life that surround us, in what is still a fragmented neighbourhood.

WIDER INITIATIVES

Because we wish to be open and to meet people where they are, providing them with the necessary tools and know-how to take hold of the opportunities which present themselves, we have during the last five years stimulated ten small businesses. We believe that we have improved the educational prospects for a number of local people. In 1991 fifteen people involved in the project went on to higher education, and some entered degree courses.

In 1989 I was asked to be responsible for the conception and development of, and fundraising for, a £1 million mental health project, locally called Open House and part of Mind, the mental health charity, in Tower Hamlets. This facility was opened by Lord Ennals, the President of Mind, in 1993.

The Centre has supported a number of internationally known artists and some have undertaken major commissions in Britain and abroad. Paula Haughey carved a sculpture for the BP Building in Brussels. Sheena McKinley, working in stained glass, produced the new window for St Giles' Church in Cripplegate in the City of London. Manda Hellal, one of our potters, is at present on sabbatical leave, working with a top sculptor in India. Frank Creber, our artist-in-residence, painted the head-boards, on the theme of nature and people, for the new unit for mothers and children with AIDS at Mildmay Hospital in Hackney (see Chapter 7).

On a wider front, in 1992 I became Mental Health Act Manager responsible with others for patients forced to remain at the Royal London Hospital because they might be a danger either to themselves or to other people. New plans were in the air to redevelop the traditional Victorian buildings of St Clements Hospital and move the mentally ill to the Mile End hospital site. A group of managers became increasingly concerned about this decision and within weeks prepared an alternative plan entitled 'A vision of the future of mental health in Tower Hamlets'. This plan gained the support of both political parties in Tower Hamlets but was resisted by the District Health Authority and the Royal London Hospital Trust for what we saw as short-term financial gain. We witnessed thousands of pounds of public money being channelled into meetings with professional health workers with little clear vision of what alternative futures might be available. In the new 'purchasing provider' culture, in which the DHA was charged with exploring alternatives, collusion took place to protect the vested interest of professionals regardless of the real needs of some of the most vulnerable people in Tower Hamlets. This is a biased view, but there was a serious attempt by a small minority of people to change the culture of mental health care in the borough. This debate continues even today.

In 1993 I was asked by Sir George Young, Minister of State for Housing, to join the Board of the Tower Hamlets Housing Action Trust. This quango has, in my view, the real opportunity to improve the quality of housing in one of the poorest areas of the borough. The sum of £80 million has been allocated and the project is now up and running under the very able leadership of David Gilles (Chief Exeuctive) and Dr Michael Barraclough (Chairman). I was asked to join the Board to share more widely our experience of community development in Bromley by Bow and our involvement in high quality, cost-effective community buildings. Notwithstanding the legitimacy or otherwise of quangos, I have to admit that this very capable group of people, working with the residents, is likely to produce some first-rate housing. Whilst not perfect, this process is teaching me a great deal about larger structures and how they can be made to work effectively. Frequently Tower Hamlets has experienced mismatch between the rhetoric and action of both the main political parties and the people have paid the price. A far more rigorous assessment of the consequences of particular beliefs and decision-making needs to be undertaken if public money is to be spent more effectively in the future. The Housing Action Trust will provide an interesting experiment to see if we can be any more effective.

The McCabe Educational Trust was launched by its Patron, the Right Reverend Dr George Carey, Archbishop of Canterbury, in June 1991 at Lambeth Palace. Its first initiative was Project Sinai, which takes young people from the inner cities of Britain to the Sinai desert to experience at first hand the beauty, history and complexity of the Middle East, while at the same time helping them to discover the roots of the three monotheistic faiths that are increasingly in contention in urban Europe. This project has given our activity-based approach to education an international perspective and our first trip from Bow, which included people of eight different nationalities, proved to be a major success. In 1994 the project took ninety-two young people from contexts as diverse as Belfast, Glasgow, Toxteth in Liverpool and Sheffield. In 1995 the Trust is supporting 100 young people from London to take part in the project, as part of the Pentecost '95 celebrations.

One of our major concerns in recent years has been to develop methods of working which actively influence social policy and the integration of wider community policies. In April 1991 Jean, a young mother with two children, died after a protracted illness. In the months leading up to her death the statutory services involved had failed to organise or provide care for either her or her family, though, in my opinion, she was a member of one of the most vulnerable groups in Britain. Workers at the Centre kept a detailed record of the missing care and provided much of it themselves. Jackie, five months pregnant, would each morning go in to bathe Jean. As a result of a report, written by Allison Trimble, following Jean's death, an enquiry was called in the Board Room of the Royal London Hospital. After a series of difficult, and not always co-operative, meetings, a new pilot study was implemented based on the 'key worker' model of care which we had proposed.

From the earliest days we resisted creating a context in which people became dependent upon us or anyone else. The scale of pastoral problems that we confronted demanded that we stimulate a supportive community who would care for each other. The Church, if it is seriously engaged, can in my experience have a key role to play when so many caring agencies are dominated by professional vested interests rather than by human need. The minister or priest has few career prospects or legal responsibilities and as such can cast a critical and objective eye over the realities of care in which she or he needs to be a partner.

Perhaps our major impact has been to start a wider process, stimulating a sense of value and belonging in a local context, celebrating its richness rather than concentrating endlessly upon its many problems. All the examples mentioned illustrate major growth in the last few years. How sustainable this growth is remains to be seen. What we have developed in Bow is a particular model of social engagement which seeks to be holistic in its integrated approach. We are not asking the churches to replicate our work because this project grew within a particular context at a particular time. What we would like to share with the churches of London are a few defined insights for those congregations who hesitate on the edge of serious community involvement. We know that there are many churches in London who face the same scenario that we faced. If we are serious about exploring this ecumenical model that may be able to take us beyond the 1990s then the Church must maximise its potential to be a catalyst both for community involvement and for change. Certainly for many it will demand a radical mental adjustment but, at its simplest, it will need also to take seriously the gospel imperatives to be generous, tolerant, open and truthful with our neighbours, for we are told that love of neighbour and love of God are the two greatest commandments of all.

A THEOLOGICAL PERSPECTIVE

The design of the church in Bromley by Bow is a statement of our theology in a project which seeks to be holistic in its approach to both structures and individuals. The symbols of the Eucharist sit at the centre of our life. We hold hands and share the peace each Sunday. We break the bread and share the wine, serving each other as a symbol of our Christian community. We take bread from the cafe and light the seven-day candle, as a sign of the presence of God among us. In a fragmented and often racially tense context we seek to bring people together, to open channels of communication and to be a 'presence' in the midst of God's world. We struggle to be a parable of what the Kingdom of God may be about.

The multi-coloured triptych at the front of the church speaks of the ecumenical nature of our church life. Catholics, Anglicans, members from Free Church traditions share their lives with new members who have few church roots. We all recognise that we live in a new historical situation, in which the Church must seriously review its mission, and our concern is to reflect theologically upon this urgent matter in a concrete context. To be concerned for 'the poor' in our community is a complex matter. It is not possible to implant models developed in the Third World, we must discover our own and this is central to our mission in Bow.

How do the bread and wine shared on a Sunday relate to the children's play in the nursery, the toy library and creches, and the human drama which unfolds just a stone's throw away from the table on which they are offered? I have suggested that our physical context is not unlike the medieval cathedral, where often the liturgical centre was surrounded by the market-place of life, the cosmic drama in the midst of mundane human activity. If it is true, as I have implied, that 'we are the environments we live in', powerfully and subtly influenced by them, then the impact of all this is, I suspect, considerable upon many levels of the human spirit and particularly upon the many people who pass through this space each week.

The worshipping life of the church is no longer hidden behind oak doors and frosted glass, but can be seen from the street. The stone angels, made in the workshops, fly over the children playing in the nursery. The very liturgical space is the theatre of their play. The theologian Rubem Alves reminds us how loaded with liturgical significance children's play is, as indeed Our Lord reminded us. There are few liturgical spaces in London, I would guess, that are so central to human living.

The liturgy that we have written embodies this broad ecumenical understanding. We have taken what we consider to be the most helpful aspects of the historic Christian liturgical tradition and created our own liturgy and service book, in which children, adults and strangers can take part. We share mid-week prayer each Wednesday evening by candlelight. We have recognised that the traditional rhythm of regular Sunday worship is over in our community. This is why the church had virtually collapsed by 1984.

I see my role as minister essentially as a person who shares bread and wine and the gospel stories with those who choose to listen. There is no obligation. The church space is free and open for people to share their lives and anxieties, with no hidden agenda. If people choose to become members, as some have, that is fine. The church is very much like the workshops in this respect, open to all. As a result of this tolerant attitude the church has grown from the ten elderly members in 1984 (eight of whom have now died) to twenty-five, plus six children. There are strengths in being small, and, in a diverse local community where a third of the population come from Bangladesh, we are realistic about the size of the worshipping community. Our worship provides a focus, a hub around which both activity and our reflection can revolve.

Because of our close relationship with the community many have shared in our liturgy and have, as I explained, written their own liturgies over the years. Some of these have been of astounding beauty and understanding. The church's liturgical life is no longer a compartment separated from the wider community's life, but sits naturally in the market-place of secular East End living. For this reason we resist simplistic divisions and categories that institutions often wish to place upon us.

The Church's ecumenical vision can have no walls or partitions, for on the death of our Lord the curtain of the Temple was torn from top to bottom. We are one world, one capital city, one community, who must look together, through the glasses of our different traditions, out to the ocean which borders the islands that together we have made. The church in Bromley by Bow is drawn to the conclusion that it is only here will we discover the God whom we have seen in Christ, who always comes to us, as his parables about the Kingdom of God suggest, from the future.

Chapter Ten

ON NOT LEAVING IT ALL TO THE GOVERNMENT*

●

ERIC BLAKEBROUGH

There are good reasons to be optimistic about London. Much of the development which has taken place in the latter half of the post-war period is imaginative and good. London is a world-class city and it is holding its own in the face of competition from Paris, Frankfurt, Berlin and Rome. There are real concerns about traffic congestion in London and the fumes which threaten the health of those who live and work in the city. But tourists often remark on the size and beauty of our parks and the large number of trees in our streets. The Thames is cleaner now, and there are new walkways along the banks of the river. There is much to please the eye in London.

No amount of optimism, however, can disguise the many serious social problems which have been referred to in the preceeding chapters. It is impossible not to take a political position on these matters, because most of the issues are first and foremost matters of politics. But that does not mean that the Government is responsible for all the problems and for providing all the solutions. The business community must accept greater responsibility, and so must the churches.

With the birth of the Welfare State, many people took the view that we could discharge our responsibility to love

* © Eric Blakebrough 1995

our neighbour by the simple device of paying taxes to provide statutory services to meet everyone's needs. Apart from this being an unrealistic expectation, it was hardly a moral view and certainly it lacked both the motivation and the spirit of Christian love. Yet it was not uncommon to hear the comment made about churches engaged in community work, 'Social work should be left to the State, the churches should concentrate on the spiritual needs of people' – as if satisfying basic needs for food, shelter, clothing and medical care could ever be enough.

The gospel of Jesus Christ is more than drink and food, clothing, shelter and medicine. It is a message of God's love for everyone and of good will among all people. This gospel needs to be realised in lives characterised by loving deeds. Churches, being the focal point of Christian worship, need to demonstrate this not only in their liturgies but also in their communities.

There is greater need today, than ever before, for a more effective partnership between the Government, local authorities, non-governmental organisations and the churches. This partnership will only come about if Government offers the means to achieve it, and if the churches and other organisations respond to the challenge.

NON-GOVERNMENTAL ORGANISATIONS

There are a vast number of non-governmental organisations, previously known as voluntary bodies, operating in London. Many of these are self-help organisations whose members suffer some disadvantage and have joined together for mutual support, to campaign on behalf of themselves and others like them, and to discover new and better ways of alleviating their difficulties. In theory these organisations are self-supporting, but in practice, if they are to be effective, they require at least an office and some paid staff. These networks offer a great deal of help, sensitively given and precisely meeting the needs of their members. Best of all, volunteers can give time to clients.

Because non-statutory organisations are deemed not to be professional by some in the statutory services, they are often not properly valued and are given only derisory funding. Many of these bodies should be given a higher status and central Government should ensure that they are adequately funded. These bodies represent the proper care that neighbours should have for each other, they promote a sense of community and can offer high quality services at low cost.

Another difficulty in the relationships between local authorities and NGOs is the mismatch of cultures. Town halls circulate consultative documents and issue formidable guidelines. Then there are the assessment, monitoring and evaluation functions which occupy statutory workers. In the end, it frequently happens that the bureaucracy consumes more resources than the allocation made to providing the service.

To overcome the wasteful systems of funding through local authorities, the Government ought to appoint independent inspectors who should make initial assessments of the capability of an NGO, receive annual reports and make further inspections only as and when necessary. Too much control by local authorities wastes money, takes up time which ought to be given to clients and has a tendency to stifle innovation. In order to comply with the dictates of local authorites, NGOs can end up looking like replicas of statutory services with only marginal participation by volunteers.

Non-governmental organisations provide useful job opportunities to people needing to gain experience before pursuing a career. Such volunteers can work as trainees, doing valuable work in the community while earning a minimum wage. Others who have taken early retirement and have a wealth of experience can continue to contribute to society in a meaningful way.

On not Leaving it all to the Government

The Government should give urgent consideration to encouraging a big expansion of the voluntary sector using the expertise of well-established NGOs to provide peer evaluation. It needs to be voluntary organisations who evaluate their own sector because local authorities do not really understand the different culture and have proved unable to develop these services sufficiently. It should be emphasised that NGOs are not unprofessional. The word 'professional' in modern times has taken on too much the meaning of performing for monetary reward, and too little the meaning of vocation. NGOs employ properly qualified staff at normal rates of pay, and these staff can train volunteers to very high standards of competence. Indeed, because they specialise, NGOs can develop real expertise and avoid the top-heavy administrative structures of large statutory departments.

If implemented, the proper use of non-statutory organisations would give a new meaning to the phrase 'community care'. At present, 'community care' can mean little more than relocating existing services. Encouraging voluntary service could give citizens a sense of being involved in caring for people in their local community.

THE CHURCHES

The Bishop of London is having to consider what to do with redundant churches in some central locations in London. Movements of population have left some of these buildings surrounded by offices with few local residents. With cutbacks in library services, one or two of these redundant churches could provide some of the services which have been reduced. Some libraries no longer make newspapers and magazines available. When you are poor, you cannot afford a daily newspaper, but newspapers and magazines keep people in touch with what is going on and are a vital part of the democratic system, especially if people have access to more than one newspaper. Charitable money in educational trusts would surely be available for this purpose, and it would not bother the church if some vagrants used the facility to come in out of the rain. In addition to popular novels, reference books and even a theological section might be provided. Libraries can also be used as venues for small concerts and lectures.

Child-care facilities need to be located mainly in residential areas, but it would be worth discussing with appropriate organisations whether some child-care facilities in central London might enable more women to take jobs in the city. It would be good for children to have their imaginations stimulated by stained-glass windows and noble architecture.

Some church buildings in London are situated in what has become bedsit land. The opportunities for service here are almost limitless. People living on state benefits would greatly value a cheap launderette, a communal kitchen, showers, child-care facilities and social amenities. In some areas it would be appropriate to recruit people from ethnic minorities to give advice and support. This could lead to greater ecumenical co-operation.

The redeployment of redundant church buildings is one way in which the Church can respond to the needs of people in London, but the potential is much greater in the case of a thriving congregation which is ready to put all its resources – members and buildings – at the disposal of a local community.

The Bloomsbury Baptist Church, situated at the north end of Shaftesbury Avenue and near to Centre Point, is already a vigorous part of its local community, serving significant numbers of homeless people as well as providing for the spiritual, intellectual and social needs of church members and visitors. The Anglican Diocese of London is also active in the locality through a homeless families project in nearby Gilbert Place. The intention is to bring these two existing pieces of work together and to create a new centre on the Baptist Church site. The centre will offer practical help by means of: homes for homeless mothers and children; child-care facilities for local people; a cafe and retail outlet; training courses leading to vocational qualifications. At the heart of the centre will be an active church whose aims are: to develop a Christian vision of social issues; to organise lunch-time and evening talks and discussions; to provide a spiritual home for local students; to welcome visitors from all over the world. This major new initiative will be undertaken in partnership with all the main Protestant and Catholic churches in London.

Cardinal Basil Hume, the Bishops of London and Southwark, together with the other church leaders of London, are keen to promote discussions at present taking place about the future of London, and are planning a great ecumenical celebration on the Feast of Pentecost 1995. At a Great Banquet on Saturday at the Banqueting House in Whitehall, and at a Service of Worship at Westminster Cathedral on Sunday, Christians will rededicate themselves to work for the spiritual and social regeneration of London. To demonstrate their commitment, a fund will be established to accomplish the major new initiative at the Bloomsbury Baptist Church site. It is hoped that this project will inspire many other congregations to greater involvement in meeting the needs of their local communities.

The projects described in this book are either well established or, in the case of the Bloomsbury Baptist Church, at an advanced stage of planning. There is a danger that this might intimidate a local church which is only at the initial stage of thinking about becoming more involved in the life of their local community. There is also a danger that it might be thought that such projects depend upon charismatic leadership. The presence of a charismatic leader, or a professional community worker, might get things off to a good start, but this is by no means certain. Charismatic leaders sometimes dominate, and experts can seem to be interlopers and can inhibit the development of local people who know the attitudes and values of their own group or neighbours.

It is necessary at an early stage that a Management Committee should be formed. This is to ensure that the aims and objectives of the project are being pursued, that money is being properly accounted for and that all legal requirements are being met. It is very important that the Committee do not think that their function is to run the project. The whole point of community work is that services shall be 'dictated' by the legitimate needs and choices of clients. The Director of the project must be given adequate powers to lead the people involved in the enterprise.

It should be clear from the diversity of the projects described in the second part of this book that there is no single method appropriate to every situation. The only common feature in these projects is that the approach has been pragmatic. There has been no attempt to keep to any community work orthodoxy. Community development is about enabling people to identify their own needs and find ways to realise their own goals, but this is only a guiding principle, not a definition.

The word 'community' is used a lot in this book, but there is no single definition of the term. For example, drug users and homeless people are excluded from the mainstream of society and they come together in certain places from a wide area which may cover more than one local authority. Andrew Mawson is concerned mainly with the population in the immediate neighbourhood of his church but this is not a unified population. There are all sorts of sub-groups, different cultures and different networks within most localities. It will rarely be possible to involve everyone and it is inevitable that there will be opposition from time to time.

I recall an international conference on 'Community Approaches' to drug prevention and treatment where a speaker from Asia described a whole village coming together to deal with the problem of drugs in their community. They set up a camp and persuaded all those young people who were addicted to stay in the camp for a period of three weeks to undergo a process of detoxification. At the end of that period, the whole community held a great feast to celebrate the cleansing of their village. That, no doubt, is an example *par excellence* of a 'Community Approach', but it would only be possible in a village in Asia with a strong feeling of corporate identity. When we are talking about community work, or community regeneration, in London, we can only proceed piecemeal.

Church work should have a theological context. There will need to be a continuous exploration of the connection between the historical faith contained in the Bible and the present situation. It will probably be the role of the ordained minister to articulate the discovery of Christ in the everyday experience of the group. But this is to be an open secret, available to all who want to find, but hidden in the form of parables and signs to unbelievers (Matthew 13:34–35).

Some time ago, when Sir Clive Whitmore was at the Home Office, he asked Andrew Mawson if he would describe the key elements in his understanding of 'community regeneration'. Andrew wrote down some headings and has expanded them since. I have abbreviated his draft proposals and with his permission give them here.

TEN KEY ELEMENTS OF COMMUNITY REGENERATION

1. Successful community regeneration is by nature entrepreneurial and must have a clear sense of vision and hope as people search for the opportunities for life.

    Whilst at the centre of any group there need to be common commitments and a common vision, it would be wrong to expect everyone to adopt this vision; openness and tolerance are crucial. It is also important that people's vested interests are recognised and served, creating reasons for people to work together.

2. Regeneration must be about enabling people to grow and move on, to discover together the opportunities

that exist for both their corporate and personal futures. A first step should be to find and identify the key local community people who are potential 'community entrepreneurs'.

3. Successful regeneration is about localised communities, developing localised responses. It must then be community-led and must encourage a flexibility which crosses traditional divides. New alliances and partnerships are to be encouraged between people and groups, for new ideas do not come out of the clouds, they come from human interaction. This means that churches must more seriously engage with their local communities rather than operate as a private club seeking members.

   Any church initiative which seeks to cut across neat compartments in favour of exploring new models of engagement will have its financial difficulties. However, the omens are on our side and the new government-integrated budget for London, for example, recognises the need for a far more flexible approach. Many trusts who see the clear sense and vision of what we are attempting to do will generally be helpful. The crucial thing is that vision and ideas must come first.

4. Successful regeneration is about moving across boundaries, encouraging an integrated approach. This means taking risks. People need to think laterally, encouraging movement across the statutory/voluntary/church/private/public compartments. We're all in this together! This said, a hierarchical structure, however loose and informal it is, will be most suitable for making decisions and getting things done. It must be capable of giving people the creative space they need and room for movement, so that new initiatives do not become frustrated by rigid structures and authorities.

5. All developments that take place must be seen to be

accessible and relevant to the local community. People must be given power in an organisation on the basis of their abilities, wisdom and experience rather than any particular qualifications or status. Simple democratic forms of operation that resist the more pragmatic and sophisticated realities of managing a community initiative are likely to flounder.

6. Organic growth which enables and develops those potentialities already within the community and brings together people and resources across traditional divides is what matters. The ecumenical mission of the local church should be redefined in these terms.

7. It is crucial in regenerating any community that sufficient attention is paid to the details of people's lives and their concerns. This will mean that the pastoral concerns of both staff and users are given due regard.

    Concern for detail also means attention to the detail of the designed environment and physical space that a community uses. In many senses the designed environment in the Bow centre is not dissimilar to the medieval cathedral, the worship space raising ultimate questions surrounded by the mundane market-place of life, and constantly interacting with each other to create a truly human context in which the needs of both the flesh and the spirit can engage.

8. We must recognise the importance of truly creative responses to problems. We have attempted in Bow to take seriously the creative insights of the artistic community on our doorstep and apply them to the whole structure and philosophy of the project.

9. Community regeneration is a long-term business and continuity is crucial.

10. Finally, having found the key enablers, support them. Some form of well-structured evaluation both for individuals and the community enterprise as a whole is essential.

Professional community workers may not like Andrew's emphasis on the entrepreneurial nature of community work, nor will some approve of his belief in hierarchical structures. Andrew and I worked together for three years in the Kaleidoscope Project and he came at a time when my own entrepreneurial style was being questioned. I had experimented with trying to get consensus for every decision, but in the end I abandoned this approach because it wasted too much time and was, on the whole, ineffective. Groups need leadership, imaginative – if possible, inspired – leadership. This does not mean taking responsibility from the group, it means finding from the group the sense of direction and then leading the way. Leadership must not be confused with expertise: I am not an expert on drug use, but I know 300 clients who are!

Finally, a word about evaluation and outcomes. There is a lot of talk about these things at present, and with good reason. It is important to monitor work as it is being done. There needs to be evaluation by one's peers, to encourage one another and to see where improvements can be made. But it must be clear what it is one is trying to achieve. In the kind of work we are describing we shall be looking to see the degree of friendliness between people, we shall want to judge whether people are participating creatively in the project and whether there is evidence that social regeneration is taking place. The ultimate evaluation must be the question, 'To what extent are we fulfilling Christ's command to love one another?'